BRYAN MEADOWS
THE CAVE

HOW TO HANDLE BEING HIDDEN

* PEAK

CLIFF
(PITFALLS AND PROBLEMS)

hidden *adjective*
hid·den | \ ˈhi-dᵊn \
Definition of hidden
1 : being out of sight or not
    readily apparent : CONCEALED
2 : OBSCURE, UNEXPLAINED,
    UNDISCLOSED

* BASE

ENTRANCE

The Cave: How to Handle Being Hidden
by Bryan Meadows

© 2019, Bryan Meadows
www.bryanmeadows.com
bryan@embassychurchatl.com

Published by Embassy Advantage™

Cover Design by DNG Creative

Diagrams by Justin Hardin and Damascus Media

Editing and Research Team:
Tiffany Buckner
Stephanie Anderson
Vanessa Hunter
Glenda Giles
Stephanie Coleman

ISBN-10: 0-578-48541-9
ISBN-13: 978-0-578-48541-6

This book contains material protected under International and Federal Copyright Laws and Treaties. Any unauthorized reprint or use of this material is prohibited. No part of this book may be reproduced or transmitted in any form or by any means, electronic or mechanical, including photocopying, recording, or by any information storage and retrieval system without express written permission from the author/publisher.

Although the author and publisher have made every effort to ensure that the information in this book was correct at press time, the author and publisher do not assume and hereby disclaim any liability to any party for any loss, damage, or disruption caused by errors or omissions, whether such errors or omissions result from negligence, accident, or any other cause.

Unless otherwise noted, Scripture quotations are taken from The Holy Bible, New King James Version® (NKJV). Copyright© 1982 by Thomas Nelson. Used by permission. All rights reserved.

Scriptures taken from the NEW AMERICAN STANDARD BIBLE®, Copyright©1960,1962,1963,1968,1971,1972,1973,1975,1977,1995 by The Lockman Foundation. Used by permission.

Scripture quotations marked ESV are taken from The Holy Bible, English Standard Version®. English Standard Version are registered trademarks of Crossway®.

TABLE OF CONTENT

Introduction VII
The Etymology of a Gift 1
The Etymology of a Cave 17
The Seasons of a Gift 27
The Stages of Obscurity 35
The Gift of Obscurity 47
The Gift of Community 73
The Cave and the Gift 97
The Church and the Gift 113
Cliffs and Caves 123
The Genesis of a Gift 139
The Exodus of a Gift 151
The Revelation of a Gift 169
Mountains of Influence 203
How to Handle Being Hidden 211
Diagrams 237
    Calling and Purpose 239
    The Dynamics of a Dimension 241
    Cliffs and Caves 243
    The Purpose of Caves 249
    Depths of a Cave 253
    The Ecosystem of a Gift 255
    Age of Mega Dendra 257

INTRODUCTION

Have you ever felt overlooked? Have you ever felt hidden? Have you ever felt invisible? Have you ever felt neglected or insignificant? Have you ever felt that no matter how loud you screamed, no one could hear you? I think we all have. I know I have. We call this season the cave.

Growing up the middle child, I think I have always felt ignored or insignificant for the better part of my life. As far back as I could remember, I felt like I wasn't that important. My older brother was experiencing many firsts, and of course, because he was my parents' firstborn, he got a lot of attention. And then, the baby boy got a lot of attention because he needed immediate care. Consequentially, it seemed that I just got lost in the mix somewhere. However, this made me become very introspective, which I believe is the process that grows any introvert. When you constantly have to entertain yourself, talk to yourself or just push your focus inward, I think it, over time, evolves you into an introvert. All the same, people who are constantly forced to perform or to give their attention to people outwardly, over time, become extroverts. This means that our personalities are a product of our environments, not necessarily just our wiring or our makeup.

Me growing up with many introverted tendencies, I constantly dealt with social awkwardness. I could be in a crowd and still feel all by myself. I could be at a family reunion and still feel all alone. I could be in a great church and still feel disconnected. Through years of study, prayer and mentorship, I've come to understand that this innate

feeling wasn't bad. It pushed me into a place of personal devotion, personal development and personal discovery. I learned more about myself because I learned how to manage seasons of separation, and I believe that for the growth of every gift, there are seasons of separation, seasons of invisibility and seasons of obscurity. These seasons are just as necessary as any season, if not more. I believe that the seasons of obscurity are meant to:
1. teach you humility
2. help you grow character
3. fortify your authenticity and assignment
4. to purify you from pleasing people
5. to purge you from competition and comparison
6. to concretize your calling

I believe that the season of obscurity is a necessary complexity to grow the leader.

In this book, we will explore and explicate the season of obscurity. We will look at how being hidden is a major part of our health. We will look at the purpose of the cave, the process of the cave, the pain of the cave and the perversion of the cave.

THE ETYMOLOGY OF A GIFT

Gift:
1. something given voluntarily without payment in return, as to show favor toward someone, honor an occasion, or make a gesture of assistance; present.
2. something bestowed or acquired without any particular effort by the recipient or without it being earned.

(Source: Dictionary.com)

Bible Study Tools published the following information about the word *gift*:
"In Old Testament times a gift was customarily given for the price of a bride (Genesis 34:12). The gifts of all the wave offerings of the Israelites were given by God to the priests and their families (Numbers 18:11). Fathers gave gifts to sons before sending them away (Genesis 25:6); sons would receive inheritances from their fathers (2 Chronicles 21:3). Gifts were often given to the poor. Gifts were sometimes spiritual in orientation: gifts would be given to God (Exodus 28:38) or for service by the Levites and priests (Numbers 18:6, Numbers 18:9).

Gifts can be used to gain friends (Proverbs 19:6) or influence (Proverbs 18:16). God gives gifts to people so that they can enjoy life (Ecclesiastes 3:13). Some people boast of gifts, and then never give them (Proverbs 25:14).

In the New Testament a gift was given by the priest as an

offering to God (Hebrew 5:1). The magi presented gifts to the infant Jesus (Matthew 2:11). God gave the gift of redemption to humankind (Ephesians 2:8).
God's righteousness is a gift (Romans 5:17); God has provided for us an "indescribable" gift (2 Corinthians 9:15). Paul talks about the gifts of the Spirit (1 Corinthians 12). Those who have tasted the Heavenly gift have been enlightened (Hebrews 6:4). Paul is a servant of the gospel by the gift of God's grace (Ephesians 3:7).

In general, in Scripture the word *gift* has three senses: gifts men give to men; sacrificial offerings presented to God; and gifts God gives to men, especially in connection with salvation, righteousness, and his grace."
(Source: Bible Study Tools/ Louis Goldberg)

Our focus for this study is on the gift, and for this reason, it is imperative that we understand how this relates to us. It is important that we first establish what a gift is so that we may all understand who we are and why God responds to us the way that He does. Think about the prophet Elijah when he was in his darkest hour. Jezebel, through the mouth of one of her own messengers, sent a word to Elijah swearing that in 24 hours or less, she would have Elijah killed. What's ironic about this is, Elijah was a prophet; he was a messenger of God. However, in this heart-wrenching moment, the messenger received a message from the kingdom of darkness. Make no mistake about it. The battle was not and has never been a battle between flesh and blood, but according to Ephesians 6:12, the battle is against principalities, powers, the rulers of the darkness of this world, and against spiritual wickedness in high places. Howbeit, in that moment, fear gripped Elijah and he ran for his life. In that hour, he didn't realize that the battle was not his to fight.

The Etymology of a Gift

"And Ahab told Jezebel all that Elijah had done, and with how he had slain all the prophets with the sword. Then Jezebel sent a messenger to Elijah, saying, So let the gods do to me, and more also, if I make not your life as the life of one of them by to morrow about this time. And when he saw that, he arose, and went for his life, and came to Beersheba, which belongs to Judah, and left his servant there. But he himself went a day's journey into the wilderness, and came and sat down under a juniper tree: and he requested for himself that he might die; and said, It is enough; now, O LORD, take away my life; for I am not better than my fathers. And as he lay and slept under a juniper tree, behold, then an angel touched him, and said to him, Arise and eat. And he looked, and, behold, there was a cake baked on the coals, and a cruse of water at his head. And he did eat and drink, and laid him down again. And the angel of the LORD came again the second time, and touched him, and said, Arise and eat; because the journey is too great for you. And he arose, and did eat and drink, and went in the strength of that meat forty days and forty nights to Horeb the mount of God. And he came thither to a cave, and lodged there; and, behold, the word of the LORD came to him, and he said to him, What do you here, Elijah? And he said, I have been very jealous for the LORD God of hosts: for the children of Israel have forsaken your covenant, thrown down your altars, and slain your prophets with the sword; and I, even I only, am left; and they seek my life, to take it away.
And he said, Go forth, and stand on the mount before the LORD. And, behold, the LORD passed by, and a great and strong wind rent the mountains, and broke in pieces the rocks before the LORD; but the LORD was not in the wind: and after the wind an earthquake; but the LORD was not in the earthquake: And after the earthquake a fire; but the LORD was not in the fire: and after the fire a still small voice. And it was so, when Elijah heard it, that he wrapped his face in his mantle, and went out, and stood in the

entering in of the cave. And, behold, there came a voice to him, and said, What do you here, Elijah? And he said, I have been very jealous for the LORD God of hosts: because the children of Israel have forsaken your covenant, thrown down your altars, and slain your prophets with the sword; and I, even I only, am left; and they seek my life, to take it away.
And the LORD said to him, Go, return on your way to the wilderness of Damascus: and when you come, anoint Hazael to be king over Syria: And Jehu the son of Nimshi shall you anoint to be king over Israel: and Elisha the son of Shaphat of Abelmeholah shall you anoint to be prophet in your room. And it shall come to pass, that him that escapes the sword of Hazael shall Jehu slay: and him that escapes from the sword of Jehu shall Elisha slay. Yet I have left me seven thousand in Israel, all the knees which have not bowed to Baal, and every mouth which has not kissed him."

1 Kings 19:1-18

Elijah had been a gift. Historians and theologians don't know anything about his family, their origin or his birth, nevertheless, Elijah was God's gift to a perverted people, and he was God's gift to Himself.

We are first introduced to Elijah in 1 Kings 17 when he is predicting a drought to King Ahab. The backstory is, Ahab, who was the king of northern Israel, along with his wife, Jezebel, had turned the heart of the Jews to Baal, a false god. The encounter, according to 1 Kings 17:1, went this way, "And Elijah the Tishbite, who was of the inhabitants of Gilead, said to Ahab, As the LORD God of Israel lives, before whom I stand, there shall not be dew nor rain these years, but according to my word." In those days, it was customary for a Jewish king to be advised or even confronted by a prophet of God. So, this confrontation in itself wasn't strange, but what was unusual was God's next set of instructions to Elijah. The Lord told Elijah to hide himself.

"And the word of the LORD came to him, saying, Get you hence, and turn you eastward, and hide yourself by the brook Cherith, that is before Jordan. And it shall be, that you shall drink of the brook; and I have commanded the ravens to feed you there. So he went and did according to the word of the LORD: for he went and dwelled by the brook Cherith, that is before Jordan. And the ravens brought him bread and flesh in the morning, and bread and flesh in the evening; and he drank of the brook."

1 Kings 17:2-6

Elijah had been a gift, but undoubtedly to King Ahab, Elijah was an unwelcomed gift. In other words, the king rejected God's gift. So why would God tell a gift to hide himself? Ecclesiastes 3:1-8 answers this question for us. It reads, "To every thing there is a season, and a time to every purpose under the Heaven. A time to be born, and a time to die; a time to plant, and a time to pluck up that which is planted; a time to kill, and a time to heal; a time to break down, and a time to build up; a time to weep, and a time to laugh; a time to mourn, and a time to dance; a time to cast away stones, and a time to gather stones together; a time to embrace, and a time to refrain from embracing; a time to get, and a time to lose; a time to keep, and a time to cast away; a time to rend, and a time to sew; a time to keep silence, and a time to speak; a time to love, and a time to hate; a time of war, and a time of peace."

God is Almighty. Why wouldn't He just rain fire from Heaven on Ahab and Jezebel and raise up a godly king in his place? Let's deal with the first question. Why would God tell a gift to hide himself? Let's consider how we are (or will be) as parents. If you are a parent, every dangerous thing in

The Etymology of a Gift

your house should be locked away, put away or placed on a platform so high that your children can't reach it. For example, think about a revolver. Your reason for having a gun, more than likely, is to protect your family. Nevertheless, the very gun set aside to protect your family could kill your family if it fell into the wrong hands. It doesn't have to fall into the hands of an enemy; the wrong hands can be the hands of someone who's too immature to understand its power. So, for this reason, you put away everything that could pose a threat. Your knives are safely tucked away in a knife drawer. Your tools are locked away in your tool shed. Chemicals used for staining, cleaning, pest control, or disinfecting are hidden away in cabinets, pantries and garages. Every one of these items are useful to you, but you only utilize them when you are in need of them. Those same items and chemicals that help you to run your home could prove to be fatal to your children. The same is true for God's leaders. The same prophets, apostles, evangelists, teachers and pastors that God has raised up or will raise up to lead His people to safety could prove to be counterproductive if they are released into ministry before they are mature enough to manage their mantles.

So, why did God tell Elijah to hide himself? The answer to this question is threefold:

1. **God always warned a king before He judged a kingdom.** Let's consider the prophet Nathan. He'd confronted and rebuked King David in 2 Samuel 12 for having had Uriah, the Hittite, killed so that David could continue his affair with Uriah's wife, Bathsheba. The purpose of a warning was to provoke the king to repentance.
2. **The people were not mature enough to receive Elijah or the words he'd spoken.** The Jews at that time were religiously and faithfully serving Baal. They'd already killed off many of God's prophets. For

this reason, they needed more than just a Word from the Lord, they needed an encounter with Him.
3. **Elijah was not mature enough to handle the backlash he'd receive for his decision to obey God.** This was evident in his choice to run and hide himself in a cave the moment he received a threat from Jezebel.

God had initially told Elijah to hide himself because it was his season for obscurity. He needed more development before he embraced his next assignment, but the second time he'd hidden himself, he'd done so out of fear.

So, Elijah was a gift to God's people—a gift who God had commanded in 1 Kings 17 to hide himself. By the time we get to 1 Kings 19, we see Elijah taking it upon himself to hide yet again, but this time, without the counsel of God. So, why didn't God bless and provide for Elijah when he hid himself from Jezebel the same way He'd blessed him when he'd hidden himself at the Lord's command? When God told Elijah to hide himself, it was simply because He wanted to prepare him for the next assignment. Of course, He wanted to protect His prophet as well, however, the main reason was preparation. But when Elijah received the threat from Jezebel in 1 Kings 19, he hadn't sought the Lord for his next set of instructions. Instead, he went and hid himself. A gift does not have the right to give itself, himself or herself away. A gift is the property of the gift-giver—the individual who owns the gift. Elijah was not only running from Jezebel, but he was running from his assignment. This is the very same sin that Jonah would commit some one hundred years later.

What is the etymology of a gift? The following was taken from the Online Etymology Dictionary:
"Sense of 'natural talent' (regarded as conferred) is from c. 1300, perhaps from earlier sense of 'inspiration, power

miraculously bestowed' (late 12c.), as in the Biblical gift of tongues. Old English cognate gift is recorded only in the sense 'bride-price, marriage gift (by the groom), dowry' (hence gifta (pl.) 'a marriage, nuptials'). The Old English noun for 'a giving, gift' was giefu, which is related to the Old Norse word. Sense of 'natural talent' is c. 1300, perhaps from earlier sense of 'inspiration' (late 12c.)."
(Source: Online Etymology Dictionary)

Let's look at some of the gifts spoken of in the Bible.
1. **We have the gift of life.** "And the LORD God formed man of the dust of the ground, and breathed into his nostrils the breath of life; and man became a living soul" (Genesis 2:7). Jeremiah 29:11 also states, "For I know the thoughts that I think toward you, saith the LORD, thoughts of peace, and not of evil, to give you an expected end."
2. **Sons and daughters are gifts to their parents.** "See, children are an heritage of the LORD: and the fruit of the womb is his reward" (Psalm 12:3).
3. **A wife is a gift to her husband.** "And the LORD God said, It is not good that the man should be alone; I will make him an help meet for him" (Genesis 2:18). Proverbs 18:22 states, "Whoever finds a wife finds a good thing, and obtains favor of the LORD."
4. **Jesus is God's gift to sinners.** "For God so loved the world, that he gave his only begotten Son, that whoever believes in him should not perish, but have everlasting life" (John 3:16).
5. **The Holy Spirit is a gift to believers from God.** "And I will pray the Father, and he shall give you another Comforter, that he may abide with you for ever; even the Spirit of truth; whom the world cannot receive, because it seeth him not, neither knoweth him: but ye know him; for he dwelleth with you, and shall be in you" (John 14:16-17).

6. **Ministers of the five-fold are a gift from God to His people.** "And he gave some, apostles; and some, prophets; and some, evangelists; and some, pastors and teachers; for the perfecting of the saints, for the work of the ministry, for the edifying of the body of Christ: Till we all come in the unity of the faith, and of the knowledge of the Son of God, to a perfect man, to the measure of the stature of the fullness of Christ: That we from now on be no more children, tossed to and fro, and carried about with every wind of doctrine, by the sleight of men, and cunning craftiness, whereby they lie in wait to deceive; but speaking the truth in love, may grow up into him in all things, which is the head, even Christ: From whom the whole body fitly joined together and compacted by that which every joint supplies, according to the effectual working in the measure of every part, makes increase of the body to the edifying of itself in love" (Ephesians 4:11-16).
7. **God has give His children spiritual gifts.** "Now there are diversities of gifts, but the same Spirit. And there are differences of administrations, but the same Lord. And there are diversities of operations, but it is the same God which worketh all in all. But the manifestation of the Spirit is given to every man to profit withal. For to one is given by the Spirit the word of wisdom; to another the word of knowledge by the same Spirit; to another faith by the same Spirit; to another the gifts of healing by the same Spirit; to another the working of miracles; to another prophecy; to another discerning of spirits; to another divers kinds of tongues; to another the interpretation of tongues: But all these worketh that one and the selfsame Spirit, dividing to every man severally as he will" (1 Corinthians 12:4-11).
8. **Natural fathers give gifts to their children.** "And

their father gave them great gifts of silver, and of gold, and of precious things, with fenced cities in Judah: but the kingdom gave he to Jehoram; because he was the firstborn" (2 Chronicles 21:3). Proverbs 13:22 also states, "A good man leaves an inheritance to his children's children: and the wealth of the sinner is laid up for the just."
9. **We have talents, which are low-level gifts.** "For the kingdom of Heaven is as a man travelling into a far country, who called his own servants, and delivered unto them his goods. And unto one he gave five talents, to another two, and to another one; to every man according to his several ability; and straightway took his journey" (Matthew 25:14-15).
10. **We are a gift of God for Himself.** "And God said, Let us make man in our image, after our likeness: and let them have dominion over the fish of the sea, and over the fowl of the air, and over the cattle, and over all the Earth, and over every creeping thing that creeps on the Earth" (Genesis 1:26).

YOU ARE A GIFT. The reason we must establish this is so that you can embrace and experience the full depth and potency of who you are and why you've come to be. And because you are a gift, you don't have the right to give yourself away. Yes, you have the ability to share yourself with others, but you do not have the right to give yourself away. Elijah could not give himself to obscurity; he was a gift to God's people and as such, he was supposed to wait for his next set of instructions.

Here are a few properties of a gift:
1. A gift is voluntarily transferred, either temporarily or permanently. This means that it must first be the possession of one individual, but it is then transferred from the original owner to another individual

through a medium called favor.
2. A gift is tangible or evident. I cannot give you something that you cannot experience, feel and/or use.
3. A gift has value. If I gave you a candy bar that only cost me fifty cents, I have still given you a gift, despite the fact that I didn't spend much on the gift. Nevertheless, a gift worth giving is one where a sacrifice is involved.
4. A gift has purpose. Again, let's think back to the candy bar. The purpose of the candy is to satisfy your hunger or, at minimum, your sweet tooth.
5. The gift-giver receives no compensation for the gift given. While we can exchange gifts, it is important to note that anytime a gift has strings or motives attached to it, it is not a gift, it is bait.
6. A gift is covered. In other words, a gift's potential is often concealed. For example, this book has a cover. The cover conceals the book's content; it also tells you the purpose of the book, the author of the book, and in some cases, the price you'll have to pay to get the full benefits of the book.

YOU HAVE A GIFT. Most people aren't aware of this, especially if their gifts are not evident. There are two levels of gifts. They are spiritual gifts and natural talents. Natural talents are low-level gifts. 1 Corinthians 12:4-11 reads, "Now there are diversities of gifts, but the same Spirit. And there are diversities of ministrations, and the same Lord. And there are diversities of workings, but the same God, who worketh all things in all. But to each one is given the manifestation of the Spirit to profit withal. For to one is given through the Spirit the word of wisdom; and to another the word of knowledge, according to the same Spirit: to another faith, in the same Spirit; and to another gifts of healings, in the one Spirit; and to another workings of miracles; and to another prophecy; and to another discernings of spirits; to another divers kinds of tongues; and to another the interpretation of tongues: but all these worketh the one and the same Spirit, dividing to each one severally even as he will."

Natural talents, on the other hand, are transferred to you from your parents. For example, if your mother is a great singer and your dad is an amazing illustrator, chances are, you can either sing or draw—or both! Our natural talents allow us to make money or grab the attention of the people who have the keys to our next level.

GOD GIVES GIFTS! James 1:17 says it this way, "Every good gift and every perfect gift is from above, coming down from the Father of lights, with whom can be no variation, neither shadow that is cast by turning."

GOD LOVES GIFTS! Yes, we can be a blessing to God. Even though we don't have much to give Him, we can give Him:
1. **our praise**—God wants the first-fruits of our lips. Isaiah 43:21 reads, "This people have I formed for myself; they shall show forth my praise."
2. **our will**—our will is our decisions. In short, we don't do as we want, but instead, we choose to serve the Lord.
3. **our time**—whatever we deem to be important to us, God wants. This includes our time.
4. **our bodies**—"I beseech you therefore, brethren, by the mercies of God, to present your bodies a living sacrifice, holy, acceptable to God, which is your spiritual service. And be not fashioned according to this world: but be ye transformed by the renewing of your mind, and ye may prove what is the good and acceptable and perfect will of God."

5. **our hearts**—"But seek ye first his kingdom, and his righteousness; and all these things shall be added unto you" (Matthew 6:33).
6. **our children**—Hannah prayed for a son after suffering through barrenness. She promised God that if He would give her a son, she would give him back to the Lord. God answered her prayer, and she gave birth to the prophet Samuel. She honored her end of the agreement as well.
7. **our wealth**—this is why we give God the first-fruits of our increase. Even though God doesn't want our money, He wants us, and He knows that anything that isn't tithed, be it time, money or space, has the potential to become an idol in our lives.
8. **our burdens**—Amazingly enough, wealth can be a burden if we don't have the wisdom to manage it. A burden is anything that causes you to sin, to doubt God, to worry or to tempt others.
9. **our attention**—God often called the patriarchs of old to Himself. He would have them to climb mountains just to have an encounter with Him. At the top of the mountain, the man of God couldn't focus on anything else but God.
10. **our loyalty**—"No man can serve two masters: for either he will hate the one, and love the other; or else he will hold to the one, and despise the other. You cannot serve God and mammon" (Matthew 6:24).

Note: Anytime man gives God an acceptable gift, his act is called worship.

YOUR GIFT WILL MAKE ROOM FOR YOU. This includes both your natural and your spiritual gifts! All the same, we often forget that God has given us gifts in the form of five-fold ministers. Ephesians 4:8-16 reads, "Wherefore he saith, When he ascended on high, he led captivity captive,

<u>And gave gifts unto men.</u>
(Now this, He ascended, what is it but that he also descended into the lower parts of the earth? He that descended is the same also that ascended far above all the heavens, that he might fill all things.) <u>And he gave</u> some to be apostles; and some, prophets; and some, evangelists; and some, pastors and teachers; for the perfecting of the saints, unto the work of ministering, unto the building up of the body of Christ: till we all attain unto the unity of the faith, and of the knowledge of the Son of God, unto a fullgrown man, unto the measure of the stature of the fulness of Christ: that we may be no longer children, tossed to and fro and carried about with every wind of doctrine, by the sleight of men, in craftiness, after the wiles of error; but speaking truth in love, we may grow up in all things into him, who is the head, even Christ; from whom all the body fitly framed and knit together through that which every joint supplieth, according to the working in due measure of each several part, maketh the increase of the body unto the building up of itself in love."

In short, your gift (apostle, prophet, evangelist, pastor or teacher) can and does make room for you, and will bring you before great men if you are a son or daughter of the house! This is the *law* of inheritance!

Also note that gifts can be accepted, just as they can be rejected. Gifts can be given with a cheerful heart, or they can be given grudgingly. Gifts can have strings (motives) attached to them or they can be given in love. Gifts can be or appear to be worthless in one season, but become invaluable in the next. Great examples include wine and antiques, both of which increase in value over time. Gifts can be devalued in one region, but honored in another. For example, a souvenir is worthless in its own region; it becomes valuable once the person who purchased it takes it to another region.

Additionally, Jesus was not honored in His own hometown, but when He went to other regions, He was honored and welcomed.

There's a wealth of information to learn about gifts and gift-giving, but the most important note for you to take and write upon the doorpost of your heart is—you are an invaluable gift, regardless of who sees your worth! If you're in the wrong region or the wrong season, you may very well be in a cave. The cave is a place of rest and development.

As we journey on throughout this book, you will come to better understand your role as a gift and a creative, and you will come to better understand how to appreciate and maximize every cave experience that God calls you into!

See Calling and Purpose Diagram (Page 239)

THE ETYMOLOGY OF A CAVE

"cave (n.)
'a hollow place in the earth, a natural cavity of considerable size and extending more or less horizontally,' early 13c., from Old French cave 'a cave, vault, cellar' (12c.), from Latin cavea 'hollow' (place), noun use of neuter plural of adjective cavus 'hollow,' from PIE root *keue- 'to swell,' also 'vault, hole.' Replaced Old English eorðscrafu.
cave (v.)
early 15c., caven, 'to hollow something out,' from cave (n.). Modern sense 'to collapse in or down' is 1707, American English, presumably from East Anglian dialectal calve 'collapse, fall in and leave a hollow,' which is perhaps from Flemish and subsequently was influenced by cave (n.). Transitive sense by 1762. Related: Caved; caving. Figurative sense of 'yield to pressure' is from 1837."
(Source: Online Etymology Dictionary/ Cave)

Caves have always been a source of mystery, not just because of how they're made, but because of what's been found in them. Ancient jewelry, artifacts and weapons have been found in caves. The Dead Sea Scrolls were found in a series of twelve caves. The skeletal remains of people, both small and great, have been discovered in caves. This is not surprising since, in the biblical days, caves were often used as tombs. All the same, to this day, there are families and tribes all around the world who are still living in caves.

Not to belabor the point, we will only focus on the

metaphoric use of the word *cave* in this chapter, however, our grasp or understanding of a natural cave will help us to better understand the points made in this presentation. Before we go any further, let's look at the life of a woman by the name of Emily Dickinson.

"**Emily Elizabeth Dickinson** (December 10, 1830 – May 15, 1886) was an American poet. Dickinson was born in Amherst, Massachusetts into a prominent family with strong ties to its community. After studying at the Amherst Academy for seven years in her youth, she briefly attended the Mount Holyoke Female Seminary before returning to her family's house in Amherst.
Some argue that Dickinson lived much of her life in reclusive isolation. Considered an eccentric by locals, she developed a noted penchant for white clothing and became known for her reluctance to greet guests or, later in life, to even leave her bedroom. Dickinson never married, and most friendships between her and others depended entirely upon correspondence.
While Dickinson was a prolific private poet, fewer than a dozen of her nearly 1,800 poems were published during her lifetime.

In 1845, a religious revival took place in Amherst, resulting in 46 confessions of faith among Dickinson's peers. Dickinson wrote to a friend the following year: 'I never enjoyed such perfect peace and happiness as the short time in which I felt I had found my savior.' She went on to say that it was her 'greatest pleasure to commune alone with the great God & to feel that he would listen to my prayers.' The experience did not last: Dickinson never made a formal declaration of faith and attended services regularly for only a few years. After her church-going ended, about 1852, she wrote a poem opening: 'Some keep the Sabbath going to Church, I keep it, staying at Home.'

The Etymology of a Cave

During the last year of her stay at the Academy, Emily became friendly with Leonard Humphrey, its popular new young principal. After finishing her final term at the Academy on August 10, 1847, Dickinson began attending Mary Lyon's Mount Holyoke Female Seminary (which later became Mount Holyoke College) in South Hadley, about ten miles (16 km) from Amherst. She was at the seminary for only ten months. Although she liked the girls at Holyoke, Dickinson made no lasting friendships there."
(Source: Wikipedia/ Emily Dickinson)

Emily Dickinson was an example of what we call a gift, and she is the perfect example of what happens to gifts when they choose to give themselves to caves. Even though she was an extraordinary woman, she wouldn't share herself with a community of like-minded people for too long. Instead, she was an introvert who enjoyed the serenity of seclusion, and while many of us can definitely relate to her desire to just stay at home and minimize all human contact, we must also understand that we are not our own. In other words, we have to constantly enlarge our territories by creating and joining as many communities as we can.

Ms. Dickinson was like many prophets and prophetic types today. She had a gift, and while that gift was good, it could have still been even more developed. All the same, had she stayed connected with the outside world at large, her work would be even more recognized than it is today. This is evident by another story detailed in Wikipedia regarding the introverted poet. It reads, "In the late 1850s, the Dickinsons befriended Samuel Bowles, the owner and editor-in-chief of the *Springfield Republican*, and his wife, Mary. They visited the Dickinsons regularly for years to come. During this time Emily sent him over three dozen letters and nearly fifty poems. Their friendship brought out some of her most intense writing and Bowles published a few of her poems in

The Etymology of a Cave

his journal. It was from 1858 to 1861 that Dickinson is believed to have written a trio of letters that have been called 'The Master Letters'. These three letters, drafted to an unknown man simply referred to as 'Master', continue to be the subject of speculation and contention amongst scholars" (Source: Wikipedia/ Emily Dickinson).

When Ms. Dickinson connected with someone in her arena, her gift increased. The article says it this way, "Their friendship brought out some of her most intense writing and Bowles published a few of her poems in his journal." The reason for this is, a gift is only as big as the lives it's touched. If your gift has only reached your family, your gift isn't that grand, regardless of how talented you are.

Ms. Dickinson should have made an impartation by teaching others to write poetry, howbeit, she'd fallen into the snares of what we refer to today as a comfort zone. A comfort zone is nothing but a cave that's been decorated, meaning, the person living in it has no plans to come out of it.

As a gift or a gifted person, it is important for you to know that, while God does map out windows of time for us to go into our proverbial caves, it is not His will, nor is it His intention that we stay there. After all, why would He create a gift if He intended to hide it? Luke 8:16 says it this way, "And no man, when he hath lighted a lamp, covereth it with a vessel, or putteth it under a bed; but putteth it on a stand, that they that enter in may see the light." Let's look at the makeup of a cave.

Every cave, metaphorically speaking, consists of five rooms. They are:
1. a living room
2. a kitchen
3. a bathroom

4. a bedroom
5. a hallway

Keep in mind that we are discussing the seasons and mindsets of a gift.

The living room, for a creative in a cave, is the place that he or she dwells the most. In other words, this is the gift's dominating thought. It's what drives the person. This represents the friendships, relationships and interests of the gift.

The kitchen represents the place that the gift goes to feed his or her appetite. Of course, our appetites are the results of what we feed ourselves the most. For example, what does your diet consist of? Is it gossip, slander or non-stop complaining? What type of music do you listen to? What do you fill your eye-gates with? Your kitchen consists of everything that you feed yourself.

Next, there is the bathroom. The bathroom has two primary functions:
- for the creative to relieve himself or herself
- for the creative to clean himself or herself up

A creative's bathroom reflects what he or she consumes in the kitchen. If the creative has been filling himself or herself with lies, gossip and every evil thing, the creative will experience the effects of the words he or she has spoken. This is called a storm. If the creative has been surrounding himself or herself with the right people and making the right choices, the creative will have a healthy digestive system. This means that in the solitude of a moment, the creative will reflect on every conversation he or she has had on any given day, and will extract the good from each conversation, all the while, rejecting the bad. It is here that the creative will also spend time repenting and washing himself or herself with the water of the Word.

Next, there's the bedroom. This room represents the beliefs and principles of the individual. This is where creatives go to dream, to make plans and to pray. This is where the proverbial "prayer closet" can be found. This is also where the creative goes to reproduce, not with another human being, but with his or her imaginations or, better yet, dreams. This is why Apostle Paul said, "Casting down imaginations, and every high thing that exalts itself against the knowledge of God, and bringing into captivity every thought to the obedience of Christ (2 Corinthians 10:5). In short, whatever you don't cast down or cast out of your bedroom, you lie with. This includes offense. This is why Apostle Paul also said in Ephesians 4:26-27, "Be ye angry, and sin not: let not the sun go down upon your wrath: neither give place to the devil." Anything you take to bed with you has the power to reproduce itself in your life.

Lastly, there is the hallway. This small room is often overlooked and underestimated. While architects often see hallways as wasted space, the truth is, they represent the commute or transition from one room to another, or in our case, one season to another.

What we do in each room will determine how long we stay in any given particular season. You'd be surprised at the number of people who spent their entire lives in one cave. This happens when gifts do not consult God regarding the seasons they're in, they keep rebelling against God or the gift keeps getting stuck in the seasons of transition. Think of it this way. When you were a year old, you probably couldn't reach the doorknob of your parents' bedroom. For this reason, you stood outside and cried until someone opened the door. There are some doors that creatives can't reach because they've spent the majority of their seasons demanding that other folks carry them. They won't read their Bibles, so they have to wait until Sunday to be fed the

Word of God. They won't praise or worship God enough to go into His presence, so they ride the wave of the worship team's anointing into His presence, but they are never able to sustain this when they get home. For this reason, they are still toddlers in the seasons that they should have long ago mastered and came out of. This is what it looks like to get stuck in the hallway of a cave or in a season of transition. The point is, we have to grow up to come out. The purpose of every God-initiated cave season is to mature us so that God can use us all the more.

Why does God see the need to seclude us in order to grow us up? In many cases, this is because of our environments. We are the products of what we feast on, whether it be the Word of God or gossip. Sometimes, time alone gives us the space we need to not only think for ourselves, but to hear from God. For example, most fish are indeterminate growers. This means that they grow until they die. Nevertheless, if a small fish that's supposed to grow into a large fish is placed in a small aquarium, the fish's growth will be stunted. This doesn't stop the fish's organs from attempting to grow, thus, putting pressure on the spine of the fish, and consequentially causing its untimely death. Now, get this—the cave, for you, may be your place of expansion! How so? If the people around you are living in the confines of small-mindedness, God may initiate a season of obscurity for you just so that He can recalibrate your taste buds. Consider what He did with Noah. Noah was living in the midst of sin-loving people who had no desire to serve God. Nevertheless, God orchestrated some time alone with Noah; this is why the Bible tells us that Noah walked faithfully with God. The term "walked with God" simply means he agreed with God. If the people around him were in blatant sin, we don't need a rocket scientist to tell us that Noah wasn't exactly the most popular guy in town. Nevertheless, he walked with God, and because of this, God

The Etymology of a Cave

prepared Noah for his next season.

You will never outgrow your environment! Sure, we've all had friends that we've outgrown, but this only happened because we kept reading our Bibles and seeking new revelation. Because of this, we ended up finding ourselves some new, much wiser friends. And get this, we didn't have to end any relationships, we simply fell out of agreement with the folks we once agreed with and they stopped calling us altogether! It is for this reason that God will strategically take us out of the environments that we've come to love and place us in a cave or, better yet, a season of obscurity.

To get a better understanding of how He does this, let's revisit the definition of a cave.
noun: a hollow place in the earth, a natural cavity of considerable size and extending more or less horizontally.
verb: to hollow something out.
(Source: Etymology Dictionary Online)

The word *hollow* is defined by Google as:
- having a hole or empty space inside
- without significance

Another word for *empty space* is the word *void*. In short, God will often use our voids to bring us closer to Him. He does this by using one or more of three methods:
1. **by highlighting a void or a need that's already in us.** When this happens, we'll often turn to the people around us trying to get our voids filled or, at least, get some direction. Nevertheless, when we cannot find what we're hungry for, this often provokes us to retreat into the caves God has prepared for us. From here, He is able to speak with us and address those voids. This increases our hunger for better friends and better environments.

2. **by hiding Himself from us.** This is God hollowing us out. Anytime God is hiding Himself, He's initiating a seek. And because most of us don't understand the movements of God, we can sense the void, but we don't know how to fill it. Consequentially, we attempt to fill this void with people, stuff and experiences, only to find that we still feel empty. Howbeit, at some point, we'll slow down and hear what the Lord is saying to us. It is then that we discover that what we've been chasing is far beyond our natural reach. We then begin to pursue the heart of God, thus causing us to outgrow anyone in our worlds who's running in the opposite direction.
3. **by causing us to sense our significance in places where we've been judged to be insignificant.** One of the hardest seasons for a gift to endure is one where he or she is devalued or dishonored, even though the gift is cognizant of his or her own worth. God will often hide our worth from others so that we'll know that those people aren't linked to our futures or our destinies. In some cases, He will reveal our value to others just to get them to squeeze out our potential. This is why we've had those bosses who favored everyone but us. Remember, the olive must be crushed before its oil can be released. Sometimes, God allows us to be repeatedly crushed so that our oil will be released.

We can all learn a lesson from Emily Dickinson and the many gifts out there who are just like her. The lesson in this is, we all need to have strategic times away from people so that we can spend that time with God. At the same time, the goal is to take what God gave us in the cave to the people outside of it so that they can benefit from it as well. Remember, Moses climbed Mount Sinai at the Lord's request, and it was there that he received the Ten

Commandments. He then descended so that he could share the Ten Commandments with God's people. In other words, Moses did not find a cave in the side of a mountain and make his abode there. He took on the arduous journey of ascending and descending the hill of the Lord so that God's people could reap the benefits of his cave season. This is the very thing that God wants us to do. We don't just ascend, get the revelation from God, and then, find a cave to retire in. We have to take what God has given us and feed it to His people. In other words, we are gifts, but we do not belong to ourselves! Simply put, God gave us gifts so that He could give us as gifts! Nevertheless, He develops our gifts in seasons of obscurity. It is during these seasons that He not only develops our gifts, He develops our character.

Obscurity, within itself, is a gift, even though it doesn't feel like one. Nevertheless, it is essential for the development, survival and maturing of a gift! Howbeit, the average believer despises this season. One of the main reasons believers have trouble sitting still long enough to let God develop them or their gifts is because many believers lack understanding in regards to their gifting, their wiring (makeup/nuances) and the topic of seasons as a whole. After all, we don't see these types of messages being preached in a lot of churches, and even when a leader does teach, he or she is often limited to thirty minutes to an hour of expounding. Because of this, the average believer will not sit and allow himself or herself to be developed long enough to become effective in their gifting. This is why it is absolutely important that you come to understand the seasons of obscurity.

THE SEASONS OF A GIFT

Every gift has a time. For every gift, there is a moment. There is the:
1. second of a gift
2. minute of a gift
3. hour of a gift

Second of the Gift: How long does it take a person to perceive your gift? The Bible tells us in John 4 that when Jesus was talking to the woman at the well, she perceived Him to be a prophet. So, how long does it take a person to perceive your authenticity, to perceive your assignment or to perceive your anointing? How fast can one perceive your gift?

Minute of a Gift: Usually, when you are given an opportunity, that opportunity is measured in minutes. If you have an audition, they are not going to give you all day to get your character together. You have to walk in, seize the moment, and then, you will have a few minutes to prepare yourself (make the most of the moment). Can you be effective in the time that you have been allotted? This is the minute of a gift.

Hour of a Gift: This is when your gift is most needed. Let's consider John 2. When Jesus was at the wedding at Canaan, the people wanted Him to turn water into wine. He said, "My *hour* has not yet come." This was a miracle of convenience, meaning, His gift was requested outside of its time or its hour. In John 9:4, Jesus said, "We must work the works of him that sent me, while it is day: the night cometh, when no man can work." For every gift, there is a day of the gift and there is the night for the gift. When day begins to turn into night—this is at the end of night when daybreak is on the horizon—this is the twilight of a gift. When Elijah was about to transition—when he was about to be taken up into a chariot, that was the twilight of a gift. It is during a gift's twilight that he or she will begin to transition authority. This is where and when you activate your successor, after all, every gift has a lifespan. You may be relevant now, but that doesn't mean you will be relevant forever. Just because you are popular now, doesn't mean that your popularity will continue to roll over like unused minutes on a prepaid phone. You have to reinvent yourself so that you can be relevant in another season. This is the hour of a gift.

There are four seasons of every gift. Each season coincides with a stage of a gift.
- Spring
- Summer
- Fall
- Winter

Spring: Gift Discernment: The first stage of every gift is called gift discernment. This is when you measure passion. How do you know what gift you should be focusing on? Simply put, you focus on the gift you are most passionate about. This is during the season of spring. This is considered the spring of a gift because everything is beginning to bud. Discernment usually begins with the nose; this is your ability to smell. When flowers are budding, we use our sense of smell to discern the flowers. It's the same way with a gift. When a gift hits puberty, it begins to smell itself. Every gift will go through puberty and adolescence, just like any other biological organism. And so, when your gift first starts hitting puberty, that's when you start to realize that you can produce. It is then that you start to grow and develop, and from there, you begin to get a sense of independence. I'm sure that you can now look back to the time when you were a teenager and see that you didn't know what you were doing. It is the same way with our gifts. There will come a time in your gift when you will feel like you know more than you pastor. But that's a normal stage, and any parent, be they natural or spiritual, should not get frightened or frustrated when one of their children reaches this stage. Everyone goes through that moment when they feel like they're being held back. This is okay. You are supposed to feel like that at a certain point. Just because you feel as if you are independent does not mean you can survive on your own. This is why pastoring is so important. After you have gone through it, you should be able to recognize when someone else is going through that season as well. This is the spring of a gift.

Additionally, you have to realize that whenever flowers bud, there will always be insects—these parasitic enemies, as annoying as they may be, are a part of our development. Enemies are closer during the budding of a gift than any other season. If they can destroy you in your infancy—if they can destroy you when you first start to come up, when you first start to emerge, when you first start to grow, all of these other seasons are obsolete. This is because when a gift is planted, it starts to grow roots. It has to grow down before it grows up. First the blade, then the ear, and then the full head of corn.

As a pastor, how do I know when a gift is ready to be harvested? First and foremost, you can't emerge until you are able or until you have the strength and maturity to break the surface of the soil. Dirt deals with sin. Until you can emerge from your own habit—until you can rise from the issue that keeps you down, you're not ready yet. Until you can stand up in the thing that is trying to keep you down, you still don't have the power to do ministry. Just be quiet. You are in your hidden years. If the dirt still defines you, you are still being developed. You are not ready until you are able to come up saying "I'm never going to allow depression to keep me from church again." This is breaking the surface. As long as your issues are still able to control you, you are not ready. This is the season of spring or what we call gift discernment. In gift discernment, you are measuring your passion.

Summer: Gift Discovery
Gift discovery is measuring priority. Discernment will give you a repertoire or an itemized list of all the gifts you have, but it doesn't necessarily specify which gift to use.

This is the second season. Summer is the hottest season. In the book of Matthew, Jesus gave us a parable about seeds and soil. Matthew 13:3-6 reads, "Behold, a sower went forth to sow; and when he sowed, some seeds fell by the way side, and the fowls came and devoured them up: some fell on stony places, where they had not much earth: and immediately they sprung up, because they had no deepness of earth: And when the sun was up, they were scorched; and because they had no root, they withered away." In Matthew 13:20-21, He explained this parable. He said, "But he that received the seed into stony places, the same is he that hears the word, and immediately with joy receives it; yet has he not root in himself, but endures for a while: for when tribulation or persecution rises because of the word, by and by he is offended." The heat of their assignment, the pressure of their assignment, the demand of their assignment is too much for them to bear.

Summer is there to put a demand on your gift. It is only the gift that survives under that demand that has the fortitude to survive the next season. People are going to put a demand on your gift. You can't say that you are called to prophesy if the moment someone places a demand on your gift, you back out by saying that you need more time to prepare. Again, people are putting a demand on your gift. The only way that your gift can mature and move into the realm of dependability, you have to be able to meet the demand. This means that every time people need to get healed, you are right there, ready to pray, lay hands or fast. You can't make excuses, otherwise, the rhythm of your demand is going to be off. There are going to be times when people are not going to call you because they cannot depend on you, but if you establish and meet the demand, every single time people need you, they will know that you are dependable. Your gift builds a reputation. This is the summer of a gift. This is the hot season. You have to be able to handle the heat. Your gift has to handle the heat. In short, this is the season of high demand; this is your season of high visibility. Please note that there are more storms in the summer than any other season. This is because, during this time, hot air tends to mix with cold air, which of course, causes turbulence. During this time, you are measuring priority. Can your gift withstand the heat or withstand the demand?

Fall: Gift Development: After you have discernment, you have gift discovery. After you have gift discovery, you have gift development. This is when you measure pain. Again, when we say gifts, we are not just talking about talents, we are talking about the overall chemical compound of your calling. God is not trying to get you to do something, He is trying to get you to become someone. This is a truth that you have to settle within yourself. You are moving into destiny, not a vocation. This is why you have to stop falling in love with occupations or with the view or the image of what you think your future looks like. You may be what God called you to be, but it may not be the way God called you to be it. And if you create this false image, you will fall into the snare of idolatry. In other words, you want what God has for you as long as it looks a certain way. So, most of us will reject what God has for us because it doesn't look like what we want it to look like, and this is why most of us are still waiting for something or someone. The promise came, but it did not look like what we wanted it to look like. Get this—you may have to do what you don't like until the season comes when you can do what you do like. This is how we master and manage the seasons of our gifts. Every actor knows that he or she is going to be working tables for a while. And this is a good season of development, because if you can't learn to entertain the five guests that you have at a table, how are you going to entertain five hundred people or a thousand people? If you are faithful over a few things, God will make you ruler over much. But you have to learn to manage every season.

How are my gifts being developed? The problem with the church is that we normally only emphasize gifts that are external, for example, singers, dancers, prophets and so on. But there are people who are gifted in character. All giftings are not external. Some people are gifted at interpersonal skills. I know people who can make you feel like you are the only person in their life, even when you are but a stranger.

How does the church discover or discern those gifts? We have gift development. How is your gift being developed?

Winter: Gift Deployment: This is when you measure performance. In the winter, some of the most dominant mammals hibernate. Because within the ecosystem of every gift, there has to be rest. God will initiate times of rest, either voluntarily or God will initiate times of rest involuntarily. He will raise up a Jezebel to send you into a cave so that you will have a time of reevaluation. He'll raise up a problem. He'll raise up the Mennonites to send Gideon into a cave. He'll raise up a Herod to send Jesus into Egypt. This is so that there can be a time of reevaluation. This is called gift deployment. Before a gift is deployed, before anything goes out, it goes back in.

How do you manage every season? Every season must be managed well. How you manage this particular season will determine the next season of development.
Every season is not comfortable. For example, when I first started, my major passion was martial arts. Because I loved martial arts, my friends and I used to make these Avant-garde martial arts type movies, and we used to record each other. Because we were doing film and movies, I got into video. After that, I started acting. Between all of this, I felt a call to ministry. There are some sub-categories, of course. I used to write poetry, I wrote scripts, I did a little acting, and then, I got into ministry. Now, what I did not know was that the Lord was taking me through all of these caves on the Mountain of Arts and Entertainment, because each one of them have a language. Each one of them have a culture. Each one of them has a frequency. What I mean by frequency is that I can talk and do certain things that communicate with martial artists. In film and video, I see things a certain way. When I read scripture, I see the words a certain way. I am able to setup my messages in a unique way. In other words, I am going to stack my gift. I am going to take all the things that I am good at and layer them in one presentation.

The voice of the Lord is as the voice of many rushing waters. It begins to touch every part of a human being. If you stop trying to be good at one thing and realize that everything that you have been through has value, meaning, you can stack your gifts. Use everything that you are good at. You have more than you think you know.

You can stack your gift with someone else's. You may have a talent that can be stacked with someone else's. You can make a lot of money if you stop trying to be great in one area and you stop devaluing the small places that God has placed you. You stack what you've learned, and it makes you better. Don't throw it away. The vision is yet for an appointed time.

See The Ecosystem of a Gift Diagram (Page 255)

THE STAGES OF OBSCURITY

Imagine being shipwrecked on an island where the residents have no connections to modern society. The locals welcome you to the island and provide a small hut for you to stay in, but this does little to ease your frustration, after all, your ship has been totaled and has sunk into the ocean. To add insult to injury, you didn't have a satellite on board to notify anyone of your ship's location or fate.

On the island, you find all types of precious stones, including rubies, diamonds and onyx. Howbeit, to the residents, the treasures you've discovered are considered trash. This would be welcomed news if you had a way to return to the States with your newfound riches, but you don't. Instead, you find yourself in possession of something valuable with no one to affirm its worth. So, you go out of your way to help the residents of the island to understand the value of the gems, but to no avail. To them, they're just rocks.

Now, imagine that you were that diamond. You can feel the warmth of the man's hands who's just picked you up. Maybe this time, someone will see just how valuable you are. But all of a sudden, the man draws back and throws you with all of his might towards a tree. Upon impact, you realize that you've hit a coconut. The coconut falls out of the tree and doesn't land too far from where you've landed. The hungry man then walks past you and picks up the coconut. What type of devil would cause him to prefer a wild drupe over you? How is it that he can't see your value, even though the sun radiated your glory just seconds before he tossed you into a tree full of what some consider to be over-sized nuts? The truth is, you've been hidden. Like Elijah, you are in a season of obscurity.

God hides gifts in the same manner that many Westerners hide presents from their children. These presents are concealed until an appointed time (Christmas, birthday, graduation, etc.). Because you are the gift in question, it is not uncommon for you to feel forgotten, devalued, overlooked or unimportant. What's even more frustrating is the fact that you can sense your value. Even though you've discounted yourself many times and you've attempted to give yourself away to a few people, something in you would not allow you to continue to settle. You found yourself feeling restless, constricted and depressed, so you opened your mouth and tried to convey your worth to the people around you. Nevertheless, to them, you were just another human being. Trapped in a season of obscurity, you found yourself hidden in plain sight, battling rejection, abandonment and anxiety. Before we delve more into this lesson, let's understand what it means to be in a season of obscurity.

Obscurity:
    1. the *state* of being difficult to see or understand.
    2. the *state* of being unknown or forgotten.
    3. shrouded in or hidden by darkness.
    4. to conceal or hide by or as if by covering
(Source: Merriam-Webster)

The Online Etymology Dictionary published the following definitions of the word *obscure*:
adj: 'c. 1400, "dark," figuratively 'morally unenlightened; gloomy,' from Old French obscur, oscur 'dark, clouded,

gloomy; dim, not clear' (12c.) and directly from Latin obscurus 'dark, dusky, shady,' figuratively 'unknown; unintelligible; hard to discern; from insignificant ancestors,' from ob 'over' (see ob-) + -scurus 'covered,' from PIE root *(s)keu- 'to cover, conceal.'
verb: early 15c., 'to cover (something), cloud over,' from obscure (adj.) or else from Middle French obscurer, from Latin obscurare 'to make dark, darken, obscure,' from obscurus."

When God wants to hide a thing, He conceals or covers it. For example, Proverbs 18:22 states, "Whoever finds a wife finds a good thing, and obtains favor of the LORD." The word *find* is paradoxical to the word *hide*. This means that in order for a wife to be found, she must first be hidden—or a better way to say this is, her identity must be concealed. While in her season of obscurity, it is the role and responsibility of the wife-to-be to remain hidden. This is no easy task, especially during the season when she starts to realize her value. Like a diamond on a deserted island, she may find herself hoping that she may be able to find someone to value her or, at minimum, she'll be able to convince some man of her worth. Howbeit, if she abandons her post, she will expose herself to the world prematurely. Consequentially, she may find herself in a string of failed relationships. This is why Song Of Solomon 8:4 reads, "O daughters of Jerusalem, I adjure you: Do not arouse or awaken love until the time is right" (Berean Study Bible). During her season of concealment and obscurity, she has to endure and overcome the feelings of rejection, being ignored and even feeling devalued. All of these feelings are a normal part of her development, so it is important for her to not be led by her feelings. Instead, she must resolve within herself to be led by the Spirit of God. But of course, in order for this to happen, it is imperative that she understands where she is; she has to understand that God *intentionally* hid her. Her obscurity is not from the devil; her obscurity is not a punishment for some sin in her past. She's simply being developed for her next role, whether that role be a wife, an author, an entrepreneur, a politician or a performer. Like many other gifts, she's being developed in darkness.

Once upon a time, during the era of the film camera, photographers used darkrooms to develop their snapshots. After taking a picture, they couldn't see what the image looked like because it had to be developed. The photographer had to be very patient and very meticulous, otherwise, he ran the risk of ruining the images. He would take the film into a darkroom and cut each image into separate pieces called negatives. Darkrooms were completely dark, minus a subtle red light (for black and white photos), or a green light (for color photos). These lights were used to illuminate the work area to prevent the images from being overexposed. The better photos, however, were developed in complete darkness. The images had to be taken through a process, including being placed in a small tub of water mixed with chemicals, hung out to dry and kept in darkness for a specified time. This a snapshot of what God does with His people. He hides every gift to be revealed at the appointed time or season. The problem is that nowadays, most people don't realize that they are gifts. For this reason, the average Christian overexposes himself before his time. Most Christians will not endure the process needed to equip them for their next role or assignment. Consequentially, we are seeing a rise in underdeveloped, immature believers who *feel* that they are ready to lead families, churches, companies and organizations. Hear me—in the season of concealment, one of the strengths they were supposed to develop was gaining authority over their feelings. Any believer who is led by his or her feeling is not fit to lead.

The Stages of Obscurity

On the opposite end of the spectrum of obscurity is revelation. The word *revelation* comes from the Greek word *apokalupsis*, which is where we get the word *apocalypse*, and it literally means: to uncover or an uncovering. It also means to unveil or to reveal. Where do we find the prophecy regarding the apocalypse? In the Book of Revelations, of course. Contrary to popular belief, the apocalypse doesn't just mark the end of the world as we know it; it represents the birth of a new Heaven and a new Earth (see Revelation 21:1). It's all a matter of perspective. Revelation is when the images on the film in the darkroom are now clear and can handle the light of day. They've survived the darkness and the process needed, and now, many of those photos have survived the tests of time and have become family heirlooms. Of course, darkrooms, while not so popular, are still in use today. What you take out of the darkness will determine what happens to you in your next season. Consider the story of Esther's promotion.

"So it came to pass, when the king's commandment and his decree was heard, and when many maidens were gathered together to Shushan the palace, to the custody of Hegai, that Esther was brought also to the king's house, to the custody of Hegai, keeper of the women. And the maiden pleased him, and she obtained kindness of him; and he speedily gave her her things for purification, with such things as belonged to her, and seven maidens, which were meet to be given her, out of the king's house: and he preferred her and her maids to the best place of the house of the women. Esther had not showed her people nor her kindred: for Mordecai had charged her that she should not show it. And Mordecai walked every day before the court of the women's house, to know how Esther did, and what should become of her. Now when every maid's turn was come to go in to king Ahasuerus, after that she had been twelve months, according to the manner of the women, (for so were the days

The Stages of Obscurity

of their purifications accomplished, to wit, six months with oil of myrrh, and six months with sweet odors, and with other things for the purifying of the women;) Then thus came every maiden to the king; whatever she desired was given her to go with her out of the house of the women to the king's house. In the evening she went, and on the morrow she returned into the second house of the women, to the custody of Shaashgaz, the king's chamberlain, which kept the concubines: she came in to the king no more, except the king delighted in her, and that she were called by name. Now when the turn of Esther, the daughter of Abihail the uncle of Mordecai, who had taken her for his daughter, was come to go in to the king, she required nothing but what Hegai the king's chamberlain, the keeper of the women, appointed. And Esther obtained favor in the sight of all them that looked on her. So Esther was taken to king Ahasuerus into his house royal in the tenth month, which is the month Tebeth, in the seventh year of his reign. And the king loved Esther above all the women, and she obtained grace and favor in his sight more than all the virgins; so that he set the royal crown on her head, and made her queen instead of Vashti."

Esther 2:8-16

There's so much to be learned about Esther's process, but first, keep this in mind: there is a *state* of obscurity and a *stage* of obscurity. The word *state* is defined by Merriam-Webster as "condition of mind or temperament." It is the paradigm of a person at any given time. The state of a person's mind can be witnessed in the actions they take or the words they choose. Let's review some of Esther's states throughout the many changes she had to endure.

STATE ONE: First, she was taken to a strange place (the king's castle) and placed in the custody of Hegai, the king's eunuch. This means that she had to leave behind everything that was familiar to her. Additionally, she had to go from receiving all the attention from her older cousin and caretaker, Mordecai, to being in the company of many women.

STATE TWO: She had to win the favor of a eunuch. In the season of obscurity, you may find yourself having to receive your next set of instructions from impotent people. For example, you may be far more qualified for a position on your job, but because of the season you're in, you may find yourself under the supervision of someone who is far less qualified for the position. Your job, in that hour, isn't to outdo them or show the boss that you're more qualified for the job—the key to your next level is in your ability to humble yourself.

STATE THREE: Esther may have gone from living a life of introversion to suddenly being surrounded by her competitors, and if that wasn't frustrating enough, she now had seven maidens following her around. As a gift, you can't give yourself to seclusion, even if you are introverted. A time will come when you may find yourself thrust outside of your comfort zone with no hope for return. This means you'll receive a one-way ticket to your next level, and from there, you may have to adjust to a lifestyle that you once abhorred.

STATE FOUR: Esther had to conceal her identity. As a gift, you may want to tell people who you are or what you're called to do, but doing so could prove to be a dangerous move on your part. This means that God may bring you out of your cave, all the while, charging you to conceal your identity for a season. To do this, you need to be both humble and patient.

The Stages of Obscurity

STATE FIVE: Esther had to go through twelve months of purification, meaning, she could see the prize, but she couldn't touch it. This requires discipline, faith and above all, patience.

STATE SIX: Esther's turn finally came to go before the king, meaning, she got to sample her destiny. Nevertheless, when her turn was over, like the other women, she had to go to the concubines' quarters. Sure, we know that King Ahasuerus placed the royal crown on Esther's head and appointed her as his queen, but what we do not know is how much time passed between their visitation versus her ordination.

After she'd been crowned as queen of Persia, Queen Esther's days in obscurity were far from over. As a matter of fact, they'd just begun. Once Esther was in place, destiny called. Through a series of communications with Mordecai via one of the king's chamberlains, Hatach, the queen suddenly discovered why she'd had to endure all of the seasons of obscurity and the warfare she'd endured. She learned that Haman, the king's vizier, had concocted a plan to kill all of the Jews in Persia, and her husband had authorized the decree. Of course, the queen still hadn't revealed the fact that she was a Jew to her husband. Thankfully, she'd obeyed her cousin, Mordecai, and kept her identity concealed. This turned out to be a strategic, Kingdom move on their part.

When Mordecai sent a message back to Esther, petitioning her to go before the king and speak with him on behalf of the Jews, she was hesitant. In that time, it was illegal for anyone, including the queen, to barge into the king's chambers without an appointment. She told Mordecai that the king had not sent for her for thirty days. This means that she had come out of obscurity, only to be placed in another season of obscurity. She had to be placed in another season of development so that she could be prepared for the warfare that was soon to come. Of course, if you know the rest of the story, Queen Esther followed Mordecai's instructions, and because of her faithfulness, humility and patience, she was able to save the Jews.

We all find ourselves in different states, but the word *stage* simply means how long we stay in those states. What if I told you that the stages of obscurity are the same stages that scientists call "the stages of grief?"

In 1969, a Swiss-American psychiatrist and pioneer by the name of Elisabeth Kübler-Ross (1926-2004) published a book entitled *On Death and Dying*. This book had been inspired by her work with terminally ill patients. Along with her co-author, David Kessler, the two penned a model that is still being used by grief counselors, therapists and scientists today. Together, the two penned what is now known as the Kübler-Ross Model, better known as the five stages of grief. The five stages of grief are:
1. Denial
2. Anger
3. Bargaining
4. Depression
5. Acceptance

This model was introduced to help us better understand the process of healing after a loved one has passed away, however, the five stages of grief are also used by psychiatrists to help recent divorcees. It goes without saying that we can also apply this model to the ending of any given season. And while scientists and social-behaviorists report that some people actually skip some of these stages, this theory has helped them to publish articles, theories and books that have advanced modern medicine as we know it today. When a friendship ends, we endure this process, when a relationship ends, we endure this process, when we've been terminated from a job, we endure this process and when we leave a church, we endure this process. In short, we journey from denial to acceptance, and once we reach the stage of acceptance, we are able to exit one season and enter another. Howbeit, the average Christian gets stuck in one of these stages, and for this reason, the average believer repeatedly gets stuck at the exit doors of any given season.

Let's think of a stage this way. Imagine that each stage was a platform that you stood on. On the first stage, you stood there, interacting with your audience, denying everything that they could clearly see. During phase two, you stood on the platform of anger and voiced your rage to every person who decided to hear you out. Instead of listening to your audience, you're now yelling at them. When you stepped onto the third stage, you decided to try a different approach. You're now speaking to folks you wouldn't ordinarily speak to, and you're now accepting advice that shouldn't be considered. You're now in the bargaining stage, and in this stage, you're pretty much willing to make a deal with the devil if it'll help to restore an ounce of your dignity and help you to stop feeling the pain associated with loss. When you step onto the fourth stage, you have very little to say to your audience, and they have very little to say to you. Instead, during this phase, you are speaking more inwardly. "What's the purpose of living if I can't have_____? Why even try to do the right thing? Who cares about me? No one obviously." During this phase, your friends are nowhere to be seen and you spend more time in reflection than you do in any other frame of mind.

Lastly, there is the stage of acceptance. When you step onto this stage, your countenance is now illuminated. This is your moment of revelation. This is the stage where you've come to accept the new changes in your life, you've forgiven everyone in that season and you've heard and accepted your next set of instructions from the Lord.

Which stage are you on in the season you're in? If you can't identify where you are, you'll stay there longer than you should. Are you still angry with someone for leaving you? Are you still planning to outshine the folks who rejected you? Are you still trying to make a deal with the devil? Where are you? Another way to think of it is, you're standing at the foot of a mountain, and the peak of that mountain is called Acceptance or Revelation. There are varying levels of that mountain, all of which, you'll find caves. There is the cave of denial, which is at the very bottom of the mountain. Next, there is the cave of anger, which is about three thousand feet above sea level. As you continue to ascend, you have to stop and rest in some of these caves. You spend a few months in anger, and after that season is up, you ascend five thousand feet above sea level where you find the cave of bargaining. You spend one to two months there before ascending towards the cave of depression. Once you reach this stage or cave, you realize that it's a lot bigger than the rest of the caves, so you end up staying there far longer than you should. To get you out of this cave or stage, God sends a couple of rescuers to your aid. He sends a counselor to lure you out of the cave, a deliverance minister to pull the cave and its occupants out of you, and finally, He sends a leader to help you reach the top. These are your multitude of counselors. These are the men and women who'll help you to reach the peak of acceptance. Once you stand on this summit, you have entered the revelation of that season. From there, it's time for you to enter a new season, after all, the journey does not end until you have accomplished everything God has designed you to accomplish or until you have given up (whichever route you choose).

THE GIFT OF OBSCURITY

"You ruined my life!" This is the sound that many American parents are familiar with. This is the rebuttal of the average American teenager who's come to a pivotal season in his or her development called puberty. It is during this stage that many teens believe they're old enough, mature enough and responsible enough to be entrusted with more freedom, more privacy, more money and less responsibility. It is during this phase that the child has become the biggest threat to his or her own future, oftentimes, because of peer pressure. In the midst of his anguish, a son may say within his own heart or, in some cases, aloud, "I can't wait until I turn 18! I'm leaving this place and never coming back!" And he means it. In this very upsetting moment, he believes himself to be right and his parents to be oppressive slave-masters who are obsessed with making his life as difficult as they can. But it is in this era of a child's development that most parents give their children one of the best gifts they can give them—they give them the gift of obscurity. This is the season when the word "no" seems to echo the loudest; this is the season when many teens see their parents as their enemies. Guess what? They're not entirely wrong in this because, as a parent, we have to become the enemies of who our children are trying or pretending to be so that we can cultivate them into the men and women of God that they're created to be. So, in the heat of another disciplinary moment, we have to punish our children yet again by telling them to go to their rooms, taking away their cellphones and forbidding them from talking to their friends. In this

The Gift of Obscurity

moment, we give our children a gift that they do not want or understand. In this moment, we turn off every other voice that's been influencing them so that they can hear and learn to respect the three most important voices they'll ever hear:
1. our voices
2. their own thoughts
3. the voice of the Holy Spirit

This is the wilderness season for many teens, and while it doesn't often last any more than one to a few days, it is often enough to make a notable impact in our children's decision-making. Obscurity, while frowned upon, is vital to the development of a healthy and sane person. One of the sacrifices that parents have to make in that season of their children's lives is the friendship aspect of their relationship. It is during this season that most teens believe they either dislike or hate their parents. This is because they are experiencing an assembling of all of their emotions, some of which they've never experienced before. In this hour, parents find themselves in the midst of a choice. Do I take the risk and let my child experience everything he or she wants to experience or do I stand by my convictions and say no? Most parents stick by their convictions and endure every threat to run away, every "bad parent" accusation and every manipulation attempt that their children can conjure up. For the parent, this season can last several years, but the long term benefits are well worth it, after all, there is a season of redemption. This is the season of revelation; this is the moment when most children realize why their parents made the choices they made. Ironically, God has had to endure the same behaviors from us. We've threatened to run or turn away from the faith, we've accused Him of being a not-so-caring Father, and we've tried to manipulate Him with tears, wordy prayers, the silent treatment, and through our many rebellious attempts to change His mind. Despite our many outbursts, our Father often responds by giving us the gift of obscurity. Again, this may not look or feel like a gift at all, but once we're older and more mature, we'll enter our seasons of revelation. It is during these seasons that we'll come to understand why we had to go through everything we've gone through. Let's consider the life of a joey (a baby red kangaroo).

The gestation period of a red kangaroo is just 34 days. After the joey is born, it is the size of a baby lima bean. Amazingly enough, even though the baby kangaroo leaves the womb, it is still considered an embryo. When it first exits the mother's womb, the embryo is both blind and deaf, but this doesn't exempt it from its role in its own survival. The joey then has to find its way to its mother's pouch. It must use its forelimbs (during this stage, its hind-legs are useless) to climb about six inches until it reaches its mother's pouch. This climb can take anywhere from three to five minutes. Once the joey is inside its mother's pouch, it finds a nipple and latches onto it. The embryo will continue to hold onto that same nipple for 34 weeks. Once the 34 weeks are up, it will leave its mother's pouch, but it will continue to suckle from its mother for another four months.

During the embryonic stage, the joey cannot defend itself, and of course, even after 34 weeks, a joey is still pretty much defenseless. This is why it must remain in the obscurity of its mother's pouch until it reaches maturity. The obscurity or season of concealment is more than just the gift of life; it's the gift of protection. It protects the young marsupial and allows it the time it needs to develop. The same is true for you. While you may believe yourself to be mature in the things of God, the truth of the matter is, God may still need to develop and mature you all the more for the plans He has for you. We often measure our maturity by the plans that we have for ourselves and our ability to accomplish those plans in any given season, but God doesn't measure our readiness using that same measure of rule. Instead, He measures us by the choices we make, the speed in which it takes us to obey Him, our prayer and devotional life, our knowledge of who He is and our self-discipline.

Look at the spectrum below.

Beginning (Alpha)		End (Omega)
Genesis (Start)	Journey (Life)	Revelation (Finished line)

This spectrum doesn't just apply to life and death, it also applies to seasons. Every season has a beginning, and every season has an end. The space between both seasons is called a journey. In the biblical days, many of the patriarchs of old had to physically journey from one region to another. Hear me—God didn't have them walking hundreds of miles so that they could lose weight. He was trying to get them to:
1. shed old, outdated mindsets
2. humble themselves
3. acclimate themselves all the more with His voice
4. learn the principles of leadership
5. reach the land of maturity

Abraham's life was nothing but a journey. He reached a place in God where he could no longer be identified by the name his idolatrous father, Teran, called him. He'd been called by His Most High Father, so as He obeyed God, He shed his old identity. At the age of 99, God changed Abram's name to Abraham. In the Hebrew text, the name Abram meant "exalted" or "high father," whereas, Abraham meant "father of a multitude" or "father of many nations." As you can see, God not only changed his name, He changed his identity. Abraham journeyed to 17 places over the course of his life. Let's look at the cities he journeyed to.

The Gift of Obscurity

Cities/ Regions	Event	Scriptures
Left Ur	God told Abram to leave Ur, but He did not tell him where He was taking him. Instead, He told Abram to go to a land in which He would show him.	Genesis 11:31, Acts 7:2-4
Mesopotamia (Haran)	They dwelt here until the death of Abraham's father, Terah.	Genesis 12:1-4, Acts 7:4
Damascus	(passing through)	Genesis 15:2
Shechem (Sichem)	The Lord appeared to Abraham once again and confirmed His promises.	Joshua 24:1, Judges 9:6, 1 Kings 12:1
Bethel	Abraham came to a mountain and built his second altar.	Genesis 12:8
Egypt	Abraham lied to the king of Egypt, saying that Sarah was his sister.	Genesis 12:9-20
Bethel	Abraham and Lot returned to Bethel, where strife arose between their herdsmen and they parted ways.	Genesis 13:1-9
Hebron	Abraham built his third altar for the Lord.	Genesis 13:10-18
Dan	After four kings came to Canaan, made war with the kings of Canaan and took Lot into captivity,	Genesis 14:1-14

Cities/ Regions	Event	Scriptures
	Abraham trained 318 fighting men, returned to Dan, defeated the kings (with God's help) and rescued his nephew.	
Hobah	Abraham and his small army chased the four kings to Hobah.	Genesis 14:15, 16
Salem	Abraham met Melchizedek, the priest and king of Salem. He met the king while returning from the battle. He then gave him a tithe (tenth) of the spoils of war.	Genesis 14:17-21
Gerar	Abraham sojourned in Gerar, and it was here that he lied once again about his relationship to Sarah, but this time, to Abimelech, the king of Gerah.	Genesis 20:1-18
Beersheba	Abraham and Sarah gave birth to Isaac. Hagar and Ishmael were also sent to live in the wilderness.	Genesis 21:1-34
Moriah	Abraham received a command to take Isaac to Mt. Moriah and offer him as a burnt offering to the Lord. An angel stops him	Genesis 22:1-18

Cities/ Regions	Event	Scriptures
	before he completes the act, however.	
Beersheba	Abraham returned to Beersheba.	
Hebron	Abraham purchased the cave of Machpelah and buries his wife, Sarah there. Abraham later dies and is buried in the same cave.	

The purpose of this timeline is to help you to get a visual of what the gift of obscurity looks like. While you may not be required to move from one region to another repeatedly, you are required to repeatedly change your mind. This is how we go from glory to glory; this is how we arrive in the promised lands that our forefathers never reached. This is how we break generational curses and birth nations of men and women who will carry, not just our legacies, but the name of the Lord from one century to the next. Abraham didn't just journey from one land to the next, Abraham journeyed from one revelation to another. And anytime he entered the darkness of another season, he journeyed until he'd come to a conclusion. A conclusion is the revelation of a season; it is the "why" behind the question. It is the end of a season, the end of a lie, the end of a speculation, the revealing of a mystery and the manifestation of God's promises. Let's read the story of Joseph to see what his moment of revelation looked like.

The Gift of Obscurity

Beginning (Alpha)		End (Omega)
Genesis (Start)	Journey (Life)	Revelation (Finished line)
Joseph is thrown into a pit by his brothers and then sold into slavery.	Joseph journeys from the pit to the promise.	Joseph is second in charge of Egypt.

"Then Joseph could not refrain himself before all them that stood by him; and he cried, Cause every man to go out from me. And there stood no man with him, while Joseph made himself known to his brothers. And he wept aloud: and the Egyptians and the house of Pharaoh heard. And Joseph said to his brothers, I am Joseph; does my father yet live? And his brothers could not answer him; for they were troubled at his presence.
And Joseph said to his brothers, Come near to me, I pray you. And they came near. And he said, I am Joseph your brother, whom you sold into Egypt. Now therefore be not grieved, nor angry with yourselves, that you sold me here: for God did send me before you to preserve life. For these two years has the famine been in the land: and yet there are five years, in the which there shall neither be ripening nor harvest. And God sent me before you to preserve you a posterity in the Earth, and to save your lives by a great deliverance. So now it was not you that sent me here, but God: and he has made me a father to Pharaoh, and lord of all his house, and a ruler throughout all the land of Egypt."
Genesis 45:1-8

Can you imagine the intensity of this moment? Joseph's brothers found themselves standing in front of a man they'd once hated—a man they'd done great evil to. They'd sold him into slavery because of their unquenchable jealousy. They'd once stripped off his coat of many colors—an heirloom that his father had given him, tossed him into a pit, plotted to take his life, and had finally agreed to sell him into slavery. Of all the wicked things they'd done to him, one of the greatest insults had to be the ripping away of his coat. This was his mantle. This was his identity. Little did any of them know that the coat of many colors was prophetic in nature. It was a coat of many textures, and it represented the different places he'd go, the different offices he'd hold and how God would knit all of those together through the many struggles he'd endure. In that moment, he was the second most powerful man in Egypt (next to Pharaoh). This was a moment of revelation; this was the moment when what was once hidden was suddenly revealed. What had been revealed in this moment was Joseph's identity, and not just his physical identity, but his purpose. It was the answer to the prayers he'd lifted up while in the pit. These were the prayers he'd likely thought had been answered when he'd found himself in Potiphar's house, having been made overseer over everything Potiphar owned. It was the answer to the prayers he'd lifted up when Potiphar's wife lied on him after he'd left behind yet another mantle (his cloak) in her hands. Stripped once again of his rank, office and integrity, Joseph had found himself in prison, humbled, humiliated and bound. These were the answers to the prayers he'd lifted up from the prison—prayers that appeared to be locked in his cell with him. And there, in that moment, he was standing on an answered prayer. God had already revealed to him why he'd suffered everything he'd suffered, but he found himself standing in front of the men who'd sold him into slavery 13 years prior. Can you imagine the intensity of that moment? Can you imagine the level of fear that gripped each man in that moment? After 13 years, Joseph surely didn't look the same. He was dressed like an Egyptian and likely wearing the makeup that many

Egyptian dignitaries wore in that time. And most importantly, he was wearing a different coat, but this time, no man could take his mantle from him. He was in his place of revelation; he'd survived his season of genesis, he'd survived his many exoduses, and now, God's words echoed from from Genesis 1:3, "Let there be light." Light represents a revealing or a revelation. In the moment of revelation, what was once hidden or obscure is made manifest. In that moment, Joseph knew who he was, why he'd come to be, and how he'd come to be second in charge, next to Pharaoh. He wasn't just Jacob's son; he wasn't any of the many names his brothers had once called him. He wasn't Potiphar's secondhand man, he wasn't the ungrateful pervert Potiphar's wife had made him out to be, and he wasn't just an interpreter of dreams, nor was he Pharaoh's sidekick; Joseph was a gift from God. He had been a gift to his father, a gift to Potiphar, a gift to Pharaoh, a gift to Egypt, a gift to the Jews, and now, in that moment, he'd humbled himself and became a gift to his brothers—men who were not worthy of the grace, love and forgiveness he extended to them. In that moment, Joseph acted like Christ.

Over the course of Joseph's life, he'd had to take off several mantles, but this didn't mean that he'd lost his assignment. It meant that God had a greater plan for him. For example, he never stopped being Jacob's son, even when he was presumed to be dead. Favor hadn't abandoned him when his brothers abandoned him. Instead, the favor of God followed Joseph everywhere he went. He didn't cease to be over Potiphar's house, after all, Potiphar was Egyptian. When Pharaoh promoted him, Joseph was not only over Potiphar's house, but over every Egyptian's home. The message behind this is, a gift doesn't stop being a gift, even in its darkest hour. Let's look at Joseph's timeline again, but this time, let's focus on his journey.

Beginning (Alpha)		End (Omega)
Genesis (Start)	Journey (Life)	Revelation (Finished line)
Joseph is thrown into a pit by his brothers and then sold into slavery.	Joseph was 17 when he was sold into slavery.	Joseph is second in charge of Egypt.
	Joseph spent about 11 years in Potiphar's house.	
	Joseph spent no less than two years in prison (See Genesis 40).	
	Joseph interprets Pharaoh's dream and is promoted to second in charge, next to Pharaoh.	

Around the age of 39, Joseph's brothers came to Egypt, and he was around 41 when they came a second time. Joseph's point of revelation wasn't the moment he put his brothers to shame. Joseph's greatest promotion came when he forgave his brothers. He became the very thing he had been designed and broken to be: a gift. Joseph's assignment wasn't to hurt, harm or shame his brothers. His assignment was to reveal his identity to them, and then, reveal the love of God to them. Remember, Jacob wasn't just Joseph's father, he was the father of Joseph's brothers as well. This means that by hurting his brethren, Joseph would simultaneously break his father's heart. Why do we not understand this same concept as the body of Christ? Sure, many of our brothers and sisters in the Lord have hurt, rejected, betrayed and persecuted us, but God still loves them. This is why we are required to forgive them. Forgiveness is the revelation of a gift. It is the moment when the rejected becomes a gift to the very people who set out to harm them.

You are a gift. Throughout this book, I'm going to keep reminding you of this so that this truth can engrave itself in your DNA. You aren't just in this Earth to fulfill the cycle of life. You aren't just here to live, get saved and die. You are here to pass the baton, meaning, there is something that God wants to give you so that you can pass it on the generations that are set to come behind you. But as a gift, it is important that you understand that obscurity can also be a gift, even though many believers today see it as a curse. Hear me—your perception of a gift will determine what you do with it. Joseph's brothers sold a gift for twenty pieces of silver because they didn't know the value of it. Potiphar's wife tried to open a gift that did not belong to her. Potiphar tossed that same gift in prison, meaning, because of his perception, he could not see the value of the gift that had once been entrusted to his care. Joseph, the gift, kept being tossed around until he found himself in a place of honor. (Note: God will never leave a gift in an environment of dishonor.) Consider the parable of the talents.

"For the kingdom of Heaven is as a man traveling into a far country, who called his own servants, and delivered to them his goods. And to one he gave five talents, to another two, and to another one; to every man according to his several ability; and straightway took his journey. Then he that had received the five talents went and traded with the same, and made them other five talents. And likewise he that had received two, he also gained other two. But he that had received one went and dig in the earth, and hid his lord's money.

After a long time the lord of those servants comes, and reckons with them. And so he that had received five talents came and brought other five talents, saying, Lord, you delivered to me five talents: behold, I have gained beside them five talents more. His lord said to him, Well done, you good and faithful servant: you have been faithful over a few things, I will make you ruler over many things: enter you into the joy of your lord.

He also that had received two talents came and said, Lord, you delivered to me two talents: behold, I have gained two other talents beside them. His lord said to him, Well done, good and faithful servant; you have been faithful over a few things, I will make you ruler over many things: enter you into the joy of your lord.

Then he which had received the one talent came and said, Lord, I knew you that you are an hard man, reaping where you have not sown, and gathering where you have not strewed: And I was afraid, and went and hid your talent in the earth: see, there you have that is yours.

His lord answered and said to him, You wicked and slothful servant, you knew that I reap where I sowed not, and gather where I have not strewed: You ought therefore to have put my money to the exchangers, and then at my coming I should have received my own with usury. Take therefore the talent from him, and give it to him which has ten talents.

Matthew 25:14-28

A parable is never as it seems; it is not a straightforward story. A parable is a mystery; it is revelation hidden from those who do not have eyes to see or ears to hear, meaning, it is hidden from people who are citizens of the kingdom of darkness. Parables are spiritual lessons that were told by Jesus Christ to illustrate or demonstrate a moral standard.

In the parable of the talents, the moral of the story is, wherever honor is, grace and blessings abound, but

The Gift of Obscurity

wherever there is dishonor, the curse of lack will be upon that place. The dishonorable servant's problem wasn't just that he'd buried his talent, the problem was in the why. Why had he buried his talent? The answer is revealed in the scripture. "Then he which had received the one talent came and said, Lord, I knew you that you are an hard man, reaping where you have not sown, and gathering where you have not strewed: And I was afraid, and went and hid your talent in the earth: see, there you have that is yours."

He'd buried his talent because he had a twisted perception of his master. He could not recognize the fact that his master was a gift to him, and his master had given him a gift. Anytime a man or woman does not recognize or honor a gift, that man or woman cannot and will not reap the benefits of that gift. Let's think back to the Samaritan woman at the well. After Jesus told her that she'd had five husbands, she said to Him in John 4:19, "Sir, I perceive that thou art a prophet." Of course, Jesus was much more than a prophet, and after speaking with Him a little longer, her perception changed. She was the first Gentile to get saved. In that moment, she became an evangelist. John 4:28-29 reads, "The woman then left her waterpot, and went her way into the city, and saith to the men, Come, see a man, which told me all things that ever I did: is not this the Christ? Then they went out of the city, and came unto him."

In the parable of the talents, the unfaithful servant had simply refused to serve. He was a gift, but he'd given himself to the cave. In other words, he wasn't in a season of obscurity. Instead, he'd buried himself under a bunch of negative perceptions regarding his master, and because of this, he could not be trusted. For this reason, the talent, which is a low-level gift, was taken from him and given to the man who'd been blessed with five talents. Talents are gifts that are passed from one generation to the next. This means that the man who'd been graced with five talents was a gift to his children, grandchildren and the generations to come. This truth is backed by Proverbs 13:22, which reads, "A good man leaves an inheritance to his children's children: and the wealth of the sinner is laid up for the just."

There is a difference between a womb and a tomb. The gift of obscurity is a womb, but anytime a man or woman buries the gift that God has given them or a man or woman hides himself or herself because of fear, that individual has just entered a tomb. This is important to note because God does hide gifts, but there are some gifts who hide themselves because of fear, offense, rejection, pride or vanity.

When God places us in seasons of obscurity, it is easy for us to believe that we have somehow offended Him. It's easy for us to believe that we've fallen under a curse and that God has forsaken us. For this reason, gifts who find themselves in the pit of obscurity often find themselves in seasons of reflection. It is during these times that we replay some of the conversations we've had, we revisit some of the choices we've made, and if we're going to be honest, we question some of the spiritual connections we've made. We ask ourselves questions like, "Have I somehow linked myself up to a witch? Why does _____ call me every time I'm about to pray? Is she really saved? Did I sow seeds into bad ground? Did I make a bad move when I sowed into that prophet? Am I at the right church or did I fail to discern the voice of God once again? Who is for me? Who is against me? Is Christianity real or am I just blindly following a bunch of folks into a pit? Where are my friends? Where are my pastors? Why does it feel like God is backing my enemies? Am I outside of His will?" Hear me—this line of questioning is normal whenever you find yourself in a season of obscurity, but you should never give into the temptation to write off any of your relationships just because of how you feel. As a matter of fact, it is during this time that you need

The Gift of Obscurity

to be reaching out to the gifts who God has assigned to your life. These are your leaders, your multitude of counselors and your friends. Additionally, it is important for you to know that the season within itself is a gift.

How is the season of obscurity a gift? Let's look at a timeline of David's life.

Year	Event
1041-40 BC	Believed by theologians to be around the time when David was born.
1035 BC	Samuel anoints David as future king of Israel.
1023 BC	David serves as a minstrel to Saul, but returns to his father's house to tend the sheep. He serves Saul when requested.
1020 BC	David kills Goliath.
1015 BC	David becomes Saul's armor bearer.
1010 BC	Saul's fear of David manifests and he removes him from his court and places him as a commander in his army. This was a demotion.
1008 BC	Saul offers his daughter, Michal, to David as a wife. He intended for her to be a snare to David.
1007 BC	Because of Jonathan and Michal's warnings, David flees from Saul and hides himself in Ramah.
1006 BC	David goes on the run from Saul and hides himself in Nob, where he is helped by Abimelech, the priest. He then runs to the city of Gath. There, he pretends to be a madman.

1005 BC	David hides himself in the Cave at Adullam. He gets the opportunity to kill Saul, but instead, cuts off a corner of his robe as a warning.
1004 BC	Saul finds David in Hakilah. There, David spares the king's life once again. David flees to Gath for a second time.
1000 BC	David's mentor, Samuel, dies. Additionally, his enemy, Saul, is killed, along with his best friend, Jonathan. David is anointed king over Judah.
993 BC	David is publicly anointed king over all of Israel and Judah.
976 BC	David goes on the run when he learns that his son, Abasalom, is plotting to kill him.
961 BC	David dies and passes the baton to his son, Solomon.

Just by looking at David's timeline, we can see that, unlike Joseph, he wasn't cast into a pit of obscurity. Instead, he'd been repeatedly chased into hiding. It's important that we understand who David was. David was a gift. He was a gift to his father, but his father had not seen his value. He was a gift to his brothers, but like Joseph's brothers, they saw him as problematic. We can see the evidence of this in 1 Samuel 17:28. The narrative here is, Israel is in a cold war with the Philistines—a war that's about to heat up, and the Philistines have deployed their weapon of mass destruction: Goliath. In a brazen attempt to intimidate the Jews, Goliath repeatedly mocked the men for forty days. David's brothers were all on the battlefield, but David was at home with his father, Jesse. Jesse gave David an ephah of parched grain and ten loaves of bread. He told him to take the food to his brothers. David did as he was told, but once he got on the battleground, David felt something stirring within him. David felt righteous indignation swelling in his belly as he listened to Goliath challenge the Israelites. He then asked a few of the men who stood by him, "What shall be done to the man that kills this Philistine, and takes away the reproach from Israel? For who is this uncircumcised Philistine, that he should defy the armies of the living God?" David's brother, Eliab, heard him. He knew David's name, but he did not know his God-given identity. 1 Samuel 17:28-29 reads, "And Eliab his oldest brother heard when he spoke to the men; and Eliab's anger was kindled against David, and he said, Why came you down here? And with whom have you left those few sheep in the wilderness? I know your pride, and the naughtiness of your heart; for you are come down that you might see the battle. And David said, What have I now done? Is there not a cause?"

David's brother had reduced him in his heart to being nothing more than a sheep-herder or shepherd. He didn't understand the spiritual implications of a shepherd (Jesus is our Shepherd). Additionally, he accused him of being prideful and nosy. Nevertheless, David was a gift, and he was ready to give the people he'd someday lead their first gift. He was ready to give them the head of their enemy, Goliath. Of course, David defeated Goliath and the battle was won.

If you'll look at the timeline of his life, you'll notice that David's life had been plagued by misunderstandings. Again, David endured everything he went through because of who he was. He was a gift, and anytime God gives a gift to mankind, the enemy tries to intercept, steal or destroy that gift. We can see the evidence of this in the book of Daniel. Daniel had been fasting and praying for three weeks (21 days). Daniel 10:2-14 reads, "In those days I Daniel was

The Gift of Obscurity

mourning three full weeks. I ate no pleasant bread, neither came flesh nor wine in my mouth, neither did I anoint myself at all, till three whole weeks were fulfilled. And in the four and twentieth day of the first month, as I was by the side of the great river, which is Hiddekel; Then I lifted up my eyes, and looked, and behold a certain man clothed in linen, whose loins were girded with fine gold of Uphaz: His body also was like the beryl, and his face as the appearance of lightning, and his eyes as lamps of fire, and his arms and his feet like in color to polished brass, and the voice of his words like the voice of a multitude. And I Daniel alone saw the vision: for the men that were with me saw not the vision; but a great quaking fell on them, so that they fled to hide themselves. Therefore I was left alone, and saw this great vision, and there remained no strength in me: for my comeliness was turned in me into corruption, and I retained no strength. Yet heard I the voice of his words: and when I heard the voice of his words, then was I in a deep sleep on my face, and my face toward the ground.
And, behold, an hand touched me, which set me on my knees and on the palms of my hands. And he said to me, O Daniel, a man greatly beloved, understand the words that I speak to you, and stand upright: for to you am I now sent. And when he had spoken this word to me, I stood trembling. Then said he to me, Fear not, Daniel: for from the first day that you did set your heart to understand, and to chasten yourself before your God, your words were heard, and I am come for your words. But the prince of the kingdom of Persia withstood me one and twenty days: but, see, Michael, one of the chief princes, came to help me; and I remained there with the kings of Persia. Now I am come to make you understand what shall befall your people in the latter days: for yet the vision is for many days."

Look at the timeline here. Daniel had been fasting for 21 days, but the angel who had been released to deliver the

The Gift of Obscurity

answer to his prayer had been held up for twenty days. This means that God answered Daniel immediately, but the enemy fought against the gift that the angel was attempting to bring to Daniel. The gift was the very thing he'd been praying for. Let's revisit King David. He was the youngest child of his father, but unlike Joseph, he had not won favor with his father. Instead, there is an extra-biblical tale that attempts to explain why Jesse had not considered David to be his son.

David's mother was reportedly named Nizbeth. According to Jewish folklore, David's father, Jesse, began to doubt that he was David's biological father because he'd pretty much stopped sleeping with his wife, Nitzbeth. The backstory is, Jesse was the son of Obed. Obed was the son of Boaz and Ruth. Ruth was a Moabite. The Hebrew law stated that Jewish women could not marry Moabite men, but it did not explicitly say that Jewish men could not marry Moabite women. For this reason, Boaz married Ruth and fathered his son, Obed, with her. According to Jewish tradition, Boaz died on his wedding night, but not before consummating his marriage with Ruth. His death was believed to be the result of a curse brought on by his choice to marry a Moabite woman. This belief was supported by the fact that Ruth's former husband, Mahlon, had also passed away prematurely, along with his brother, Chilion, who had also married a Moabite woman.

After Jesse, the son of Obed, had fathered seven children with his wife Nizbeth, he began to question the purity of his own bloodline. He believed himself to be an impure man, since he was the grandson of a Moabite woman. Because he loved Nizbeth, he reasoned within himself that continuing to sleep with her was causing her to be in sin. For this reason, he decided to cease all sexual relations with her. Desiring to have a "pure" heir, he decided to do what Abraham had

The Gift of Obscurity

once done; he decided to marry his wife's Canaanite maidservant because the law allowed him to marry a female who'd converted to Judaism. The maidservant, however, loved Nizbeth and was not happy with this arrangement, so the two of them decided to switch places on what should have been Jesse's wedding night to the Canaanite woman. Of course, like his predecessor, Jacob, who'd fallen into the same trap, it is believed that Jesse had been drunk. Nevertheless, according to the tradition, the two women switched places and Jesse ended up having sex with Nizbeth who he'd, in his drunken state, thought was the Canaanite woman. During this encounter, Nizbeth had conceived David, and months later, it was discovered that she was pregnant. Because he didn't realize he'd had sex with her, Jesse believed that David was a bastard; he believed he was the illegitimate son of some other man. Jesse's sons wanted to stone their mother, but because of his love for Nizbeth, Jesse forbade them from doing so, and a few months later, David was born. For this reason, David was rejected, not just by Jesse, but also by his brothers. Again, this is an extra-biblical tale, meaning, there is no biblical evidence to support this, but it does answer the question of why Jesse had David working in the field, while his other sons enjoyed the comfort of living and working in the home, alongside their father. This theory is supported by David's prayer in Psalm 69:7-8, where he says, "Because for your sake I have borne reproach; shame has covered my face. I am become a stranger to my brothers, and an alien to my mother's children." David grew up rejected, despised and shunned; he grew up in obscurity. But David was a gift, and as such, he would go on to become the king of Israel, and Jesus would come from his lineage. David's obscurity had been a gift as well. Every time he'd been sent to the field to take care of his father's sheep, he had been preparing for his future role as king of Israel. His father's rejection of him prepared him for Saul's rejection of him. His brothers' rejection of him had prepared him for Jonathan's alleged betrayal. Theologians believe that David's prayer as recorded in Psalm 41:9 was in reference to Jonathan. In this prayer, he says, "Yes, my own familiar friend, in whom I trusted, which did eat of my bread, has lifted up his heel against me." The many years he'd spent in obscurity prepared David for the Cave at Adullam. While protecting his father's sheep, David had once killed both a bear and a lion. These two fights prepared and qualified him for his fight with and victory over Goliath. In other words, David's season of concealment had readied him for his role as king and his warfare prepared him for the many battles he'd have to fight. His rejection prepared him for his role as king, after all, any man or woman who's called to greatness won't have many friends. "It's lonely at the top, but crowded at the bottom" (author unknown). This age-old adage seems to have a ring of truth to it!

People who go out of their way to be seen, heard and accepted are oftentimes not appointed by God to lead. True leaders are developed in rejection, abandonment, betrayal and loss. Like an old black and white photo, true leaders are developed in the dark. And while the darkness is not a fun place to be, it is God's way of protecting a gift from emerging before his or her time.

You can often measure the size of the leader by the size of the warfare he or she has overcome. And while this is not a one-sized-fits-all model, we can see this template in use in many of the biblical characters who God used. For example, Abraham's father, Terah, was polytheistic, meaning, he believed in and worshiped many gods. Joshua 24:2 confirms this; it reads, "And Joshua said to all the people, Thus said the LORD God of Israel, Your fathers dwelled on the other side of the flood in old time, even Terah, the father of Abraham, and the father of Nachor: and they served other

The Gift of Obscurity

gods." Terah not only worshiped many gods, he manufactured them.

Let's look at the life of Jesus Christ. Jesus was thirty years old when He began His ministry. He was crucified at the tender age of 33. This means that Jesus ministered for a total of three years. What happened before this? Like any gift, the Lord had to go through a long process for what some would consider a very short assignment. At the age of 12, Jesus visited the Temple at Jerusalem, and from the ages of 12 to 30, He worked as a carpenter. Once He turned 30, everything seemed to accelerate in His life. During that time, He:

- ◆ met John, the Baptist, and was baptized by him in the River Jordan.
- ◆ recruited Andrew, Simon, Philip, and Nathaniel as disciples.
- ◆ Performed many miracles, including turning water into wine, healing the paralytic at the Pool of Bethesda, and so on.

Every year after this, the miracles He performed increased. This was undoubtedly because the faith of the people who'd heard of Him or followed Him had also increased. In Jesus's life, He'd found Himself in seclusion many times. One of His most famous seasons of obscurity happened after He'd fasted for forty days. Matthew 4 tells the story.

"Then was Jesus led up of the spirit into the wilderness to be tempted of the devil. And when he had fasted forty days and forty nights, he was afterward an hungered. And when the tempter came to him, he said, If you be the Son of God, command that these stones be made bread. But he answered and said, It is written, Man shall not live by bread alone, but by every word that proceeds out of the mouth of God. Then the devil takes him up into the holy city, and sets him

on a pinnacle of the temple, and said to him, If you be the Son of God, cast yourself down: for it is written, He shall give his angels charge concerning you: and in their hands they shall bear you up, lest at any time you dash your foot against a stone.
Jesus said to him, It is written again, You shall not tempt the Lord your God. Again, the devil takes him up into an exceeding high mountain, and shows him all the kingdoms of the world, and the glory of them; and said to him, All these things will I give you, if you will fall down and worship me. Then said Jesus to him, Get you hence, Satan: for it is written, You shall worship the Lord your God, and him only shall you serve. Then the devil leaves him, and, behold, angels came and ministered to him."

Matthew 4:1-11

This was one of the many seasons of obscurity that the Lord had to endure. He didn't have anyone around Him to keep Him company. The angels came and ministered to Him *after* He'd endured the many temptations of the enemy. Despite what He endured in that season, He continued to speak the Word of God because He is the living Word of God. What was happening to our Lord? He was increasing in wisdom, stature and favor with God. He was enduring some of the many temptations that would befall us. Lastly, He was teaching us how to respond to Satan when he tempts us.

"You ruined my life!" This may be your rant to the Lord today, but if you allow Him to grow you up, not just in age or in stature, but in love, you will come to better understand your journey. The journey isn't about getting you from the crib to the coffin; the journey is about:
- ◆ maturing you in love. "There is no fear in love; but perfect love casts out fear: because fear has torment. He that fears is not made perfect in love" (1 John 4:18).

The Gift of Obscurity

- ◆ replacing fear with faith. Fear is a hollow spot in the soul that's filled with vain imaginations and ungodly beliefs. What then is faith? "Now faith is the substance of things hoped for, the evidence of things not seen" (Hebrews 11:1).
- ◆ allowing God to publish your testimony before others, so they can also be encouraged.

Remember this: you are a gift, and as such, you are gifted. Additionally, as a gift, you give gifts. Oftentimes, a word in due season is a gift that keeps on giving. How many of us can remember something someone said to us that changed the trajectory of our lives? Many of us can. Lastly, everlasting life is a gift that was delivered to you through the gift who we know as Jesus, the Christ. Nevertheless, in order for you to realize and acknowledge the value of what you've been given and who you are, you have to first discover the value of obscurity. People who don't understand or respect their seasons of concealment expose themselves to the very things and people that God was trying to protect them from.

See Age of Mega Dendra Diagram (Page 257)

THE GIFT OF COMMUNITY

"Go to the ant, thou sluggard; consider her ways, and be wise: Which having no guide, overseer, or ruler, provideth her meat in the summer, and gathereth her food in the harvest."

Proverbs 6:6-8

Let's consider the interesting world of ants.
- ◆ Ants are social insects, meaning, they live and work together in organized family structures.
- ◆ The average lifespan of a fire ant is two to six years (for queens) and fire ant workers generally live between four to six weeks.
- ◆ The average lifespan of a black ant is 15 years.
- ◆ When temperatures drop below 50 degrees Fahrenheit, ants make their sanctuary in nests underground or under the barks of trees.
- ◆ Ants go into a period of suspended development during the winter months. During this time, they become sluggish. Diapause is very similar to hibernation, however, it is not just reserved for winter months. Ants go into this state anytime the environmental factors are unfavorable, such as hot, dry summers and during times of food shortage.
- ◆ Ants carry fifty times their own weight.
- ◆ Ants are farmers. For example, ants will store and protect aphids from their natural predators and shelter them in their nests so that they can have a never-ending supply of honeydew.
- ◆ Each ant has a specific job. The queen's job is to lay

The Gift of Community

eggs. All other female ant workers feed the larvae, forage for food and supplies, keep the colonies clean by taking out the trash and defend the nest. The job of male ants is simple—to mate with the queen.

In Proverbs 6:6, God tells sluggards to consider the ant. In other words, learn from the ants; study their ways and mimic them. One of the greatest strengths of an ant is its ability to work in a community. Ants are not selfish; they do not complain about their roles or wages. They simply work together, and for this reason, they are able to survive some of the harshest conditions.

As we can see, ants are highly organized, social creatures that rely on community and communication to survive. There's a really interesting fable, entitled *The Grasshopper and the Ant* (Source: Perry Index, Number 373/ Aesop's Fables). It reads, "Once there was an ant and a grasshopper. The ant worked very hard. He worked and worked all day. He made a lovely house. Every day, the ant would work and look for bread or food. Every time he got a piece of food, he would eat just a little, then save the rest for winter.
The grasshopper on the other hand, was very lazy. The grasshopper liked to sing and relax all every day. He didn't work to save food. The grasshopper would just sing and play music. He would relax in the sun. Then autumn came. The leaves were falling and all the little ants and grasshoppers were gathering food before there was no more. Ant worked very hard.
'Save your food,' warned the ant. But the grasshopper was lazy and didn't go work. 'Build a house. Winter is coming,' said the ant. But again the grasshopper ignored the ant. He just relaxed and played music in the autumn sun.
Then the days grew cold. The sun was not enough. The grasshopper needed a house to protect him from the winter. He knocked on the ant's door. 'Please let me stay in your

house for winter.'
'What were you doing all summer and autumn?' asked the ant.
'Playing music and relaxing in the sun,' said the grasshopper.
'No, you can not come in. You should have made a house,' said the ant.
'Please give me some food at least,' said the grasshopper.
'No, you should have looked for food,' replied the ant.
The grasshopper left the ant's house. He had no food and no house for the winter."

The moral of this story is, what you do today will determine what your tomorrow looks like. Nevertheless, fables are much like parables; they are designed to teach a lesson. The difference between the two is:
- ◆ only Jesus told parables
- ◆ parables were true stories used to illustrate a point
- ◆ fables are fabricated stories conjured up in the imaginations of men, written to illustrate a point

With that being said, if we were to use what we know about the Word of God and apply it to the story of *The Grasshopper and the Ant*, we could extract much more from the fable, for example:
1. The ant was organized, but the grasshopper was led by its feelings.
2. The ant had a community or church home, but the grasshopper was a free spirit.
3. The ant had wise counselors; the grasshopper refused even the counsel of the ant.
4. Preparation is the highest level of faith. Lack of preparation is the highest level of entitlement. Entitlement is just another dimension of pride. Proverbs 16:18 reads, "Pride goes before destruction, and an haughty spirit before a fall."

5. Every ant is a member of a body or organization, and while the roles and expectations of ants are unrealistic in regards to humans, the fact that each ant accepts and performs its role demonstrates a high level of intelligence. This is why ants are believed by evolutionists to be older than dinosaurs, meaning, they've survived climates and eras that have completely annihilated their much larger and more complex neighbors.

We have to understand that community, just like obscurity, is a necessary part of our development. Throughout this book, we've talked about the importance of the season of obscurity, but it is important to note that obscurity is just a season. Prophets, prophetic types, and creatives should NEVER attempt to grow in isolation. Prophetic gifts need community for a few reasons:
1. Creative people need community to understand that they aren't crazy, awkward, or weird.
2. They need accountability from people who understand their wiring and makeup.
3. They need to learn the interpersonal and social skills that are needed for their success.
4. Inspection and observation are both a part of the creative's development. People need to see you grow.

Of course, you may say that you're not a creative person, and this couldn't be further from the truth. Everyone is creative—only, some people have yet to identify their creative abilities. Hear me—even in your season of obscurity, you need a community of believers around you. This doesn't mean that they're crowding your personal space, it means that they are calling to check in with you, and it also means that you need to be accountable with them. This is how gifts avoid getting stuck in one of the many stages of any given season.

The Gift of Community

In the natural, there are four seasons, and they are:
- ◆ Spring
- ◆ Summer
- ◆ Fall
- ◆ Winter

Every season is divided into months.
- ◆ Spring runs from March 1st to May 31st
- ◆ Summer runs from June 1st to August 31st
- ◆ Fall runs from September 1st to November 30th
- ◆ Winter runs from November 31st to February 28th (February 29th in a leap year)

In the Northern Hemisphere, the seasons are different.
- ◆ Spring starts September 1st and ends November 30th
- ◆ Summer starts December 1st and ends February 28th (February 29th in a leap year)
- ◆ Fall (autumn) starts March 1st and ends May 31st
- ◆ Winter starts June 1st and ends August 31st

Every month is characterized by varying temperatures. Since I'm from Atlanta, let's look at a chart of Atlanta's average temperatures by month.

Month	Average Temperature
January	53° / 33°
February	58° / 35°
March	66° / 42°
April	73° / 49°
May	80° / 57°
June	86° / 65°
July	89° / 69°

Month	Average Temperature
August	88° / 68°
September	82° / 62°
October	74° / 50°
November	64° / 41°
December	55° / 35°

Chart Source: National Centers for Environmental Information

During the winter months, most people wear extra layers of clothing, including coats, long johns and undershirts. As the seasons change and the temperatures start rising, people wear less clothing because our bodies can overheat, just like we can suffer from hypothermia. In other words, we can utilize our feelings in a healthy way. If I feel cold, my body is telling me that it needs an extra layer of covering, I need to turn up the temperature or I need move around so that my body can produce heat.

I teach a lesson called the cosmological order of the Kingdom. If you're not familiar with this model or if you need a refresher, here is the order:
- ◆ Every world is made up of kingdoms
- ◆ Every kingdom is divided into realms
- ◆ Every realm is made up of dimensions
- ◆ Every dimension is comprised of levels
- ◆ Every level is accessed by doors
- ◆ Every door is opened by keys

For the sake of this study, we are just going to focus on kingdoms and realms.

Your natural heart, according to science, has four chambers,

The Gift of Community

which are two atria and two ventricles. The natural heart gives us a better understanding of our minds. Of course, when the Bible references the heart of man, the author is talking about the mind. Ironically enough, the Earth is divided into four hemispheres. What I'm getting at is, you are a world and you have a heart, but unlike your natural heart, your mind is divided up into three sections. These spheres or sections of your soul, biblically speaking, are kingdoms. They are your:
- mind
- will
- emotions

In every kingdom, there is a realm, and in every realm, there is a king. Every king has a temperature (temperament). With humans, our temperament is the temperature of our character. Merriam-Webster defines the word *temperament* this way: "characteristic or habitual inclination or mode of emotional response." Your habitual inclination is determined by your habitat. Merriam-Webster defines the word *habitat* as: "the place or environment where a plant or animal naturally or normally lives and grows."

In every kingdom, there is a king, and wherever there is a king, there is a throne for the king to sit and rule on. Additionally, every kingdom is divided up into domains. A domain, according to Merriam-Webster, is "a sphere of knowledge, influence, or activity."

In short, there is a ruler or king on every throne of your soul (mind, will and emotions). One of the interesting facts about kingdoms in the biblical days is that some of them were often in alliance with one another. These alliances were formed through mutual consent. Another word for mutual consent is *agreement*. This word has more of a legal connotation. In the biblical days, kings would ally themselves with other kings for one or more reasons, some of which included:

1. **Trade (produce):** In every region, there is a climate, and in every climate, there are plants and animals that flourish in that climate. This means that in one kingdom, they may have had an overabundance of apples and goats, whereas, in another kingdom, they may have had an overflow of bananas and fish. Trade agreements allowed kingdoms to enjoy foods that they ordinarily wouldn't have.
2. **Trade (humans):** Men have always loved exotic women, even in the biblical times. This is why God had to command Israel to not intermarry with pagans. Nevertheless, many kings and kingdoms enjoyed the benefits of intermarriage. For this reason, some kingdoms would link up for the sole purpose of trading women. They also traded slaves. Remember, Joseph was sold into slavery and Ahab created a trade agreement with Phoenicia and married Jezebel to strengthen that agreement.
3. **Strength:** There is strength in numbers. At least, that's what some kings believed. Abraham disproved this when he overtook four kings with a little over three hundred men whom he had personally trained. By allying themselves with other kingdoms, some kings were able to overtake other kingdoms, thus, enlarging their territories.
4. **War:** Some kingdoms came under attack, and for this reason, they allied themselves with other kingdoms so that they could defeat their enemies.
5. **Fear:** The news of another kingdom being overtaken by an opposing kingdom was enough to cause some kings to link up with their not-so-friendly neighboring kingdoms.

The kingdoms that make up your soul should all be linked

through agreement, however, this isn't always the case. This is why James 1:8 says, "A double-minded man is unstable in all his ways." The word *mind* here means soul; it means that the man has two souls or two opposing kingdoms in operation within him. There is the Kingdom of Light (God) and the kingdom of darkness. The Greek word for soul is "psuché" and it literally means "breath." In other instances, it means "heart." So, we can translate a double-minded this way:

A man with two hearts—one good and one evil. In Romans 7:21, Apostle Paul describes his dilemma this way, "I find then a law, that, when I would do good, evil is present with me."

A man with two breaths or two life forces ruling his world. Note: in the ministry of deliverance, demons often come out through breathing, after all, they are called malevolent spirits. The word *spirit* comes from the word *pneuma* which means breath. When a man goes through deliverance, he expels the demonic ruler that has been occupying a realm in his heart. If he does not give God His rightful place on that throne, the evil spirit will return, according to Matthew 12:43-45, but this time, it will bring seven spirits more wicked than itself. The words "more wicked" simply denote rank. It means that the new rulers will outrank the former one, thus, causing the man to be in a worse state than he was before the deliverance. This is why deliverance should be followed up with or preceded by counseling.

Again, in every kingdom, there are seasons. Ecclesiastes 4:1-8 reads, "To every thing there is a season, and a time to every purpose under the Heaven: A time to be born, and a time to die; a time to plant, and a time to pluck up that which is planted; a time to kill, and a time to heal; a time to break down, and a time to build up; a time to weep, and a time to laugh; a time to mourn, and a time to dance; a time to cast away stones, and a time to gather stones together; a time to embrace, and a time to refrain from embracing; a time to get, and a time to lose; a time to keep, and a time to cast away; a time to rend, and a time to sew; a time to keep silence, and a time to speak; a time to love, and a time to hate; a time of war, and a time of peace."

The questions we have to pose to ourselves daily are:
- ◆ **Is God on the throne of my mind?** In other words, is He in control of my thoughts and my choices? Do I see Him first, or do I seek the counsel of another ruler?
- ◆ **Is God on the seat of my will?** In other words, does my will match His will or am I "doing my own thing"?
- ◆ **Is God in control of my emotions?** In other words, am I driven by my feelings or do I force my feelings to bow to the Word of God?

And while each of these domains of the mind all have their own thrones, your emotions are subject to whomever it is that's on the throne of your mind, and whomever (or whatever) it is on the throne of your will. The mind is the highest level of the soul, followed by the will and then, the emotions. The mind is the head of the soul, the will is the limbs of the soul; it is where the mind expresses itself. The emotions are the health of the soul. If the mind isn't divided within itself, the individual won't make choices that conflict with his or her moral standards or beliefs. In other words, the individual will be at peace. If the mind is divided within itself, the individual will make conflicting choices in an attempt to see "what works." Again, choices are nothing but the expression of the will or whatever it is that the individual has agreed with. If the mind is unsettled, the individual's emotions will be unstable, or a better word for this is *unhealthy*. Your emotions are nothing but the weather of your belief system. If you're calm, it's because your mind is at peace with your will.

If there is a different king in the seat of your emotions than the one who's on the throne of your mind, you will wrestle with instability, frequent bouts of depression, indecisiveness and feelings of defeat. Additionally, you will always find yourself like the Apostle Paul, at war within yourself. And here's the caveat: what you may be experiencing is not warfare if two or all of the kingdoms (mind, will and emotions) are at war with one another. Instead, the fight doesn't become warfare until there is a desire, an agreement and a strategy to dethrone everything that opposes the heart, mind and will of God. In other words, warfare is about dominion; it's never a fight without a cause. The enemy will always engage in warfare when he's:

1. fighting for what he believes to be his right to a throne, either you've placed in on or your parents, grandparents or ancestors have placed him on
2. fighting to reclaim a throne that he was once occupied
3. fighting to overthrow a king or a kingdom

One of the ways to deal with a demonic ruler is, you have to break the agreements you have with him. Remember, kings often established agreements based on:

- **Trade (produce):** What is it that you are sinning to get or keep?
- **Trade (humans):** Who is it that you are sinning to get or keep?
- **Strength:** What are you battling within? This will help you to better understand why you have established some of the alliances (relationships, both platonic and/or romantic) that you've established.
- **War:** Who hurt you and why haven't you forgiven them?
- **Fear:** Who or what are you afraid of?

The Gift of Community

These are the agreements that absolutely have to be dealt with if you want to, not only enjoy "seasons" of freedom, but a lifetime of freedom.

But how does this tie into the gift that is community? In the body of Christ, there are three personality types (just like there are in the world), and they are:
1. introverts
2. extroverts (also known as extraverts)
3. ambiverts

"Introvert and extravert, basic personality types according to the theories of the 20th-century Swiss psychiatrist Carl Jung. According to these theories, an introvert is a person whose interest is generally directed inward toward his own feelings and thoughts, in contrast to an extravert, whose attention is directed toward other people and the outside world. The typical introvert is shy, contemplative, and reserved and tends to have difficulty adjusting to social situations. Excessive daydreaming and introspection, careful balancing of considerations before reaching decisions, and withdrawal under stress are also typical of the introverted personality. The extravert, by contrast, is characterized by outgoingness, responsiveness to other persons, activity, aggressiveness, and the ability to make quick decisions.
This typology is now regarded as overly simplistic because almost no one can be accurately described as wholly introvert or extravert. Most persons fall somewhere between Jung's two types—i.e., they are ambiverts, in whom introversive and extraversive tendencies exist in a rough balance and are manifested at different times in response to different situations."
(Source: Brittanica/ Science/ Introvert and Extravert)

While I agree with the large majority of this article, the truth is, most introverts are *not* shy. This is a misnomer, and modern day scientific studies back this claim. Most introverts are just socially awkward, meaning, they don't fit into society's template of normality.

The problem is, introverts tend to surround themselves with other introverts. Extroverts tend to surround themselves with other extroverts. Ambiverts surround themselves with everybody.

Extroverts
Extroverts are generally outgoing, energetic people who love being around other people. As a matter of fact, they draw their strength from relationships. One of the issues with extroverts is, they often look for affirmation in many of the relationships they build, and they draw their energy (self worth, determination, drive) from these relationships. A few famous extroverts are or were:
- Bill Clinton (former President of the United States)
- Winston Churchill (former Prime Minister of the United Kingdom)
- Muhammad Ali (boxer)
- Oprah Winfrey (talk show host/ actress)
- Mother Teresa (nun)
- Michael Jackson (artist/ performer)

Introverts
Introverts are typically reserved, stand-offish people who prefer time alone over social gatherings. Introverts are self-reliant, meaning, they have a built-in charger of sorts, but introverts lose energy (inspiration, determination, peace) whenever they're in social settings for an extended period of time. The problem with the introvert is, they often think they don't need anyone. It is for this reason that you'll find more introverts in the caves of isolation (not obscurity) than you do every other social group. Like their extroverted brethren, introverts can and do pursue affirmation, however, unlike

extroverts, if an introvert does not receive this affirmation, they are more likely to feel rejected and withdraw themselves.

A few famous introverts are or were:
- Barack Obama (former President)
- Albert Einstein (physicist)
- Bill Gates (business magnate, investor, author)
- Eleanor Roosevelt (political figure, diplomat, activist)
- Abraham Lincoln (former President)
- Warren Buffet (business magnate, investor, speaker)
- Michael Jordan (former basketball player, entrepreneur)

Ambiverts
Ambiverts fall smack-dab in the center of the extrovert-introvert spectrum. Ambiverts enjoy social gatherings, however, like their introverted brethren, need time alone to recharge. It goes without saying that ambiverts enjoy the best of both worlds. Ambiverts are oftentimes introverts with extroverted tendencies or vice versa, meaning, they tend to lean more towards one end of the extrovert-introvert spectrum than the other. For this reason, I won't list any famous ambiverts, since most celebrities are recorded as either being introverted with extrovert tendencies or extroverted with introvert tendencies.

As a creative gift, it is absolutely vital to your success and sanity that you familiarize yourself with your wiring. People who never take the time to get to know themselves usually think there is something wrong with them, and because of this, they look for help that they don't need. In other words, they try to fix what ain't broke, and they repeatedly break what God is attempting to fix in their lives. For example, extroverts rarely take time out for themselves to think or pull on the potential that God has placed within them. For this reason, they often pull on the potential of others and

The Gift of Community

even push their friends to go higher. Consequentially, this leaves them feeling used, misunderstood and underappreciated. Too much down-time can leave an extrovert feeling anxious, depressed and cranky. This is simply how God wired the extrovert. Introverts, on the other hand, spend a lot of quality and not-so-quality time with themselves and will often try to empty out all of their potential in one setting (season, locale, relationship, etc.). In other words, introverts tend to be anxious, and if something does not pan out in a small window of time, introverts will often abandon great ideas, relationships or whatever it is that they're building. Everything that God gives you does not come already put together. In other words, introverts tend to abandon things and people who have the potential to become assets to their lives when those things or people are in their winter seasons. Guess what?! Every gift has a spring and a summer as well! In other words, if they give God (the King of kings and the Lord of lords) His rightful place in their hearts, a person who appears to be a waste of space today may prove to be invaluable tomorrow!

There's nothing wrong with either typology, however, introverts need extroverted friends, and extroverts need introverted friends to live balanced lives. This is the importance of community, for example, a community of believers who come together in a church setting with one heart, one purpose and one God: YAHWEH.

"Not forsaking the assembling of ourselves together, as the manner of some is; but exhorting one another: and so much the more, as you see the day approaching."
Hebrews 11:25

An extrovert is a gift to his introverted brethren, and introvert is a gift to his extroverted brethren. Without a just balance, introverts run the risk of "becoming lovers of themselves" (see 2 Timothy 3:2) and extroverts run the risk of becoming men-pleasers (see Galatians 5:10). Both the introvert and extrovert personalities are a manifestation of God's personality. God is both extroverted and introverted. How do we know this? Let's look at the life of Jesus.

Jesus, the Extrovert
1. Jesus told His disciples to follow Him.
2. Jesus sat with tax collectors and publicans.
3. Jesus often drew large crowds.
4. Jesus went to several parties, including wedding feasts.
5. Jesus often taught in the synagogues.

Jesus, the Introvert
1. Jesus often withdrew Himself to pray.
2. Jesus went into the wilderness alone and stayed there for forty days.
3. Jesus got into a boat when a large crowd gathered while the people stood on the shore.
4. After He fed the five thousand, He sent everyone away.
5. While passing through Galilee, Jesus went through Samaria, where He came across the infamous woman at the well. He'd stayed alone while His disciples had gone into a nearby village to buy food.

As a gift, creative and Kingdom citizen, it is important for you to understand that, while Jesus lives within you, He will only dwell in the regions of your heart where He has a throne to sit on. He will give you seasons of obscurity, but He will never put you in isolation, after all, he didn't isolate Himself. He withdrew Himself when He needed to, but He did not isolate Himself.

Again, most regions have four seasons; they are:

The Gift of Community

1. Spring
2. Summer
3. Fall
4. Winter

The same is true for you. You have a soul (three kingdoms). Have you personally identified the seasons of each kingdom yet, and have you learned to identify the issues, relationships, events or habits that affect or drive each season? A simple way to do this is to create a journal. In doing so, you will find that there are certain seasons that you tend to withdraw yourself, certain seasons when you tend to surround yourself with people or, if you're introverted, certain seasons when you crave human companionship, even though you won't necessarily reach out to anyone. There are certain seasons when you endure the most warfare and certain seasons when you enjoy the spoils of war. You will also notice that in these seasons, there are periods or time slots. A period is an event that takes place within a season—one that normally precedes the onset of another event or season. For example, consider the phrase, "April showers bring May flowers." The month of April is normally a rainy month; this prepares the ground for the flowers that typically bloom in the month of May. Another example is, you may discover that you tend to form friendships, and right at the peak of familiarity, you tend to withdraw yourself from your newfound friends. This event or withdrawal is often preceded by your agitation with a system or habit you discover in your friend's life. (This trait is more-often found in extroverts.) Or you may be on the opposite end of this spectrum. You may form friendships and withdraw yourself from your newfound friends in the beginning. That is, until they share a moment of vulnerability with you. Once they show you their flaws (fears, imperfections, wounds), you may suddenly start feeling more of a personal, intimate connection with and a responsibility to them. For this reason, you may find yourself calling them more. (This trait is more-often found in introverts). This is your temperament or the temperature of your character. Learning this means that you are learning how to effectively manage your mind, will and emotions.

Let's revisit the interesting world of the ant.
- ◆ Ants live in colonies, and these communities are nothing but miniature kingdoms. While they do not have a king, every colony has a queen.
- ◆ There are certain seasons (late fall and all throughout winter) when ants withdraw themselves, but they do not withdraw themselves from their communities. They withdraw themselves from the world.
- ◆ During winter months, ants tend to be sluggish. The same is true for God's children. You may find yourself in a season where you feel sluggish, and you're not as productive as you normally are. Hear me—this doesn't mean that there is something wrong with you; it may simply mean that you are in a season of rest!

"According to a new study by researchers at the University of Lausanne, in Switzerland, worker ants that live alone have one-tenth the life span of those that live in small groups" (Source: The New Yorker/ Emily Anthes).

Other studies suggest that extroverts live longer than introverts, and while there is no scientific backing to support this claim, it is still important that both personality types form balanced communities. This means that the introvert has to force himself out of his cave, but the extrovert has to force himself into a cave. When do we need to withdraw ourselves, and when should we intermingle more? The answer is:

1. **Introvert:** you should set time aside every few days

for social networking, and while you don't necessarily have to throw a party, you should have some human interaction every few days.—and not just at church!
2. **Extrovert:** you should withdraw yourself every few days so that you can hear more from God and allow yourself to recover, heal and regroup.

Community is what makes the Kingdom, but caves allow us to spend time with the King. Community allows us to commune (fellowship) and communicate. If you find that you're overly emotional, overly anxious, always frustrated or always feeling defeated, chances are, you don't have the right community OR you're not properly utilizing the community that you have! Then again, you may be in a season when you should be withdrawing yourself! Consider this: most birds (not all) fly south for the winter! This means that our feathered friends instinctively know how to behave in each season. They're not chasing the sunshine; birds fly south because they're chasing their food supply! If we would only understand this, we would never leave good churches, nor would we sit in churches where we're not being fed!

Community is essential for the survival of a kingdom. This is supported by Ecclesiastes 4:9-12. It states, "Two are better than one; because they have a good reward for their labor. For if they fall, the one will lift up his fellow: but woe to him that is alone when he falls; for he has not another to help him up. Again, if two lie together, then they have heat: but how can one be warm alone? And if one prevail against him, two shall withstand him; and a threefold cord is not quickly broken." What can we take from this?
1. People can produce more together than they can alone.
2. Someone who falls (sin, temptation) can be helped (restored) by someone in his community.
3. People who lie together (spouses) produce heat.

Another word for heat is *friction*, and while the word *friction* is generally looked upon as a negative word, the truth is, we need friction to remain sharp (keen). Proverbs 27:17 says it this way, "Iron sharpens iron; so a man sharpens the countenance of his friend."
4. It is easier to fight and defeat an enemy with the help and support of a loved one than it is to do alone.

But how do you know who to surround yourself with versus who to withdraw yourself from?
1. **Trade (produce):** What are the people in your life bringing into your life? Love, peace, gossip or drama?
2. **Trade (humans):** Who are the people in your life connected to, and who are they introducing you to?
3. **Strength:** Are the people in your life empowering you or draining you?
4. **War:** Are the people in your life encouraging you and interceding for you, or are they arguing with you or talking about you?
5. **Fear:** Are the people in your life pushing you forward or pulling you backwards?

Understand that the people who encouraged you in your spring season may discourage you in your winter season. This doesn't mean that you have to cut all ties with them, after all, community is important to the Kingdom of God. It simply means that in that season, you have to behave like the ant and withdraw yourself from them for a season. Additionally, in the colonies or kingdoms of your heart, you are the queen (or king) ant. Everyone in your life should be helping you to build and produce. This isn't a one-way street, however. In other words, your friends and family members are the queen (or king) ants of their own lives. Your assignment is to help them reach their goals. Remember, we serve one another! Galatians 5:13 says it this way, "For, brothers, you have been called to liberty; only use not liberty for an occasion to the flesh, but by love serve one another." This means that my kingdom should be allied to your kingdom, and we should both be submitted to the King of kings and Lord of lords. In other words, unlike the grasshopper, you shouldn't be isolated somewhere, enjoying the spring and summer seasons, oblivious to the fall and winter up ahead. This is similar to what the foolish young virgins did. Matthew 25:1-12 tells the story. "Then shall the kingdom of Heaven be likened unto ten virgins, who took their lamps, and went forth to meet the bridegroom. And five of them were wise, and five were foolish. They that were foolish took their lamps, and took no oil with them: But the wise took oil in their vessels with their lamps. While the bridegroom tarried, they all slumbered and slept. And at midnight there was a cry made, Behold, the bridegroom comes; go out to meet him. Then all those virgins arose, and trimmed their lamps. And the foolish said unto the wise, Give us of your oil; for our lamps are gone out. But the wise answered, saying, Not so; lest there be not enough for us and you: but go you rather to them that sell, and buy for yourselves. And while they went to buy, the bridegroom came; and they that were ready went in with him to the marriage: and the door was shut. Afterward came also the other virgins, saying, Lord, Lord, open to us. But he answered and said, Verily I say unto you, I know you not."

Here, Jesus references the Kingdom of Heaven, but unlike *The Grasshopper and the Ant*, this is not a fable; it is a parable. The five young virgins were like the ant; they prepared themselves for the next move of God. The five foolish virgins were like the grasshopper; they were not prudent, meaning, they lived in the moment and for the moment. Consequentially, they found themselves trying to borrow the anointing, instead of just letting the Lord crush them so they could produce their own oil. This didn't work. So, when the seasons changed, they found themselves locked out of their next level, locked out of their next opportunity and locked into a perpetual season of yesterday. What went wrong? The scripture tells us that the bridegroom delayed, meaning, he didn't come when they expected him to. Guess what? Exposed women don't keep their virginity for long. Once the temperatures drop, they'll have to find heat somewhere. While this is a parable written about the state of the church (some will be ready, others won't when the Lord returns), there is a ton of revelation that can be extracted from it and applied to just about every area of our lives.

Your community is a gift and you are a gift to your community. Don't withhold yourself from the people who need you the most, and don't give yourself to any and everyone who wants to see what you're made of. Understand this: the word *community* is made up of two very powerful words: *commune* and *unity*. Communion is a powerful weapon against the enemy, and unity is a powerful weapon against the enemy. Utilize them both.

"And the LORD said, Behold, the people is one, and they have all one language; and this they begin to do: and now nothing will be restrained from them, which they have imagined to do."

Genesis 11:6

"Behold, how good and how pleasant it is for brethren to dwell together in unity!"

Psalm 133:1

"Now I beseech you, brethren, by the name of our Lord Jesus Christ, that you all speak the same thing, and that there be no divisions among you; but that you be perfectly joined together in the same mind and in the same judgment."

1 Corinthians 1:10

"For where two or three are gathered together in My name, I am there in the midst of them."
Matthew 18:20

See the Dynamics of a Dimension Diagram (Page 241)

THE CAVE AND THE GIFT

"The wealthiest place on the planet is just down the road. It is the cemetery. There lie buried companies that were never started, inventions that were never made, bestselling books that were never written, and masterpieces that were never painted. In the cemetery is buried the greatest treasure of untapped potential."
– Dr. Myles Munroe

"The graveyard is the richest place on Earth, because it is here that you will find all the hopes and dreams that were never fulfilled, the books that were never written, the songs that were never sung, the inventions that were never shared, the cures that were never discovered, all because someone was too afraid to take that first step, keep with the problem, or determined to carry out their dream."
– Les Brown

Let's take the words *grave, graveyard* and *cemetery* from the above quotes and replace them with the word *cave*. Now, let's read the revised quotes.

"The wealthiest place on the planet is just down the road. It is the *cave*. There lie buried companies that were never started, inventions that were never made, bestselling books that were never written, and masterpieces that were never painted. In the *cave* is buried the greatest treasure of untapped potential."
– Dr. Myles Munroe (revised quote)

The Cave and the Gift

"The *cave* is the richest place on Earth, because it is here that you will find all the hopes and dreams that were never fulfilled, the books that were never written, the songs that were never sung, the inventions that were never shared, the cures that were never discovered, all because someone was too afraid to take that first step, keep with the problem, or determined to carry out their dream."
– Les Brown (revised quote)

I revised the quotes to demonstrate a point, of course. The point is, there's no hope on Earth for the dead, but there is hope for the living. Right now, there are many creative gifts hiding out in caves. They've buried themselves under the weight of the world and are afraid that people will see how gifted they are. They are afraid of their own potential, so they have hidden their potential from everyone, including themselves.

The cave isn't always a bad place. As a matter of fact, we read earlier on that the first time Elijah went into a cave was because he had been sent there by God. The cave can be a place of development, a place of recovery, a rehabilitation center or a place of rest. It can be both a temporary dwelling place and a place of refuge. As a matter of fact, according to 1 Kings 18:4, a man by the name of Obadiah had taken it upon himself to hide one hundred prophets of YAHWEH from Jezebel. Jezebel had been killing off any prophet of God who refused to bow his knee to Baal. Obadiah hid the prophets in two caves. Note: According to Jewish tradition, it is believed that Obadiah received the gift of prophecy because he'd hidden the prophets of God from Ahab and Jezebel. Again, this is what is commonly known as the *prophet's reward*.

Merriam Webster defines the word *cave* three ways:
  1. a natural chamber or series of chambers in the earth

> or in the side of a hill or cliff
> 2. usually an underground chamber for storage
> 3. a place providing privacy or seclusion from others

First off, most caves are found in hillsides and/or mountainsides, even though Merriam Webster uses the term *hill*. The word *hill* is often a substitute for the word *mountain*, but the notable differences between the two are complexity and height. Most hills are easier to climb than mountains, and they aren't as tall or as steep as mountains. Mountains tend to be steeper, higher in elevation and have more climate zones. For the sake of this study, we will use the words interchangeably.

Mountains are made up of rocks and dirt. Dirt, in the scriptures, is used to represent flesh. Using this information, let's review the parable of the talents.

"For the kingdom of Heaven is as a man traveling into a far country, who called his own servants, and delivered to them his goods. And to one he gave five talents, to another two, and to another one; to every man according to his several ability; and straightway took his journey. Then he that had received the five talents went and traded with the same, and made them other five talents. And likewise he that had received two, he also gained other two. But he that had received one went and dig in the earth, and hid his lord's money.
After a long time the lord of those servants comes, and reckons with them. And so he that had received five talents came and brought other five talents, saying, Lord, you delivered to me five talents: behold, I have gained beside them five talents more. His lord said to him, Well done, you good and faithful servant: you have been faithful over a few things, I will make you ruler over many things: enter you into the joy of your lord.

The Cave and the Gift

He also that had received two talents came and said, Lord, you delivered to me two talents: behold, I have gained two other talents beside them. His lord said to him, Well done, good and faithful servant; you have been faithful over a few things, I will make you ruler over many things: enter you into the joy of your lord.
Then he which had received the one talent came and said, Lord, I knew you that you are an hard man, reaping where you have not sown, and gathering where you have not strewed: And I was afraid, and went and hid your talent in the earth: see, there you have that is yours.
His lord answered and said to him, You wicked and slothful servant, you knew that I reap where I sowed not, and gather where I have not strewed: You ought therefore to have put my money to the exchangers, and then at my coming I should have received my own with usury. Take therefore the talent from him, and give it to him which has ten talents."
Matthew 25:14-28

Remember, talents are low-level gifts that have been passed down from one generation to the next. So, let's look at the parable this way. There were three men who had inherited gifts from their parents. One man inherited five gifts; he could sing, dance, write poetry, draw and act. The other man inherited two gifts from his parents; he could make people laugh and he was a master chef. The unfaithful servant inherited one gift from his family; he was good with words. In other words, he had the gift of gab. The faithful servant went out and recorded a few albums, choreographed all of his music videos, wrote a few poetry books, started a graphic design business and he's now taking acting classes. The second guy became a famous comedian, and he launched his own cooking show. The unfaithful servant, however, went to work as a mechanic. While there's absolutely nothing wrong with this occupation, he chose this job because he wanted to have as little human contact as possible. Everywhere he went, he managed to create a cave of sorts, with his favorite cave being underneath his clients' cars. His gift of gab was supposed to be used in the pulpit, but he didn't like people. He was supposed to be winning souls, but instead, the only thing he's won is fifty dollars from a scratch off lottery ticket.

One day, each man walked into the same church and all three were eventually invited to the altar by a visiting prophet. The prophet asked each man how he'd been using the gifts God had given him. The man who'd been given five talents had won ten souls for the Kingdom of God. The man who'd been given two talents had won four souls for the Kingdom, but the man who'd been given one talent had buried his talent in his flesh. Again, the word *dirt* is used to represent flesh, therefore, the man with one talent hadn't won a single soul. Instead, he'd kept it within him. For this reason, he lost the gift of gab, and the guy with five talents found himself suddenly tapping into a gift that he couldn't trace, after all, it wasn't in his family. He became one of the most phenomenal preachers to ever live.

Do you now understand what it means to bury a gift? A gift was never designed to be hidden forever. God conceals gifts until the appointed time. Again, *you are a gift*. God can, will and does hide His gifts, but He does not bury them. To get a better grasp, we need to better understand how the Jews used caves in the biblical era.

"The most remarkable caves noticed in Scripture are, that in which Lot dwelt after the destruction of Sodom, (Genesis 19:30) the cave of Machpelah, (Genesis 23:17) cave of Makkedah, (Joshua 10:10) cave of Adullam, (1 Samuel 22:1) cave of Engedi, (1 Samuel 24:3) Obadiah's cave, (1 Kings 18:4) Elijah's cave in Horeb, (1 Kings 19:9) the rock sepulchres of Lazarus and of our Lord. (Matthew 27:60; John

The Cave and the Gift

11:38) Caves were used for temporary dwelling-places and for tombs."
(Source: Smith's Bible Dictionary)

"There are numerous natural caves among the limestone rocks of Syria, many of which have been artificially enlarged for various purposes.
The first notice of a cave occurs in the history of Lot (Genesis 19:30).

The next we read of is the cave of Machpelah (q.v.), which Abraham purchased from the sons of Heth (Genesis 25:9, 10). It was the burying-place of Sarah and of Abraham himself, also of Isaac, Rebekah, Leah, and Jacob (Genesis 49:31; 50:13).

The cave of Makkedah, into which the five Amorite kings retired after their defeat by Joshua (10:16, 27).
The cave of Adullam (q.v.), an immense natural cavern, where David hid himself from Saul (1 Samuel 22:1, 2).

The cave of Engedi (q.v.), now called `Ain Jidy, i.e., the "Fountain of the Kid", where David cut off the skirt of Saul's robe (24:4). Here he also found a shelter for himself and his followers to the number of 600 (23:29; 24:1). "On all sides the country is full of caverns which might serve as lurking-places for David and his men, as they do for outlaws at the present day."

The cave in which Obadiah hid the prophets (1 Kings 18:4) was probably in the north, but it cannot be identified.
The cave of Elijah (1 Kings 19:9), and the "cleft" of Moses on Horeb (Exodus 33:22), cannot be determined.
In the time of Gideon the Israelites took refuge from the Midianites in dens and caves, such as abounded in the mountain regions of Manasseh (Judges 6:2).

Caves were frequently used as dwelling-places (Numbers 24:21; Cant. 2:14; Jeremiah 49:16; Obadiah 1:3). "The excavations at Deir Dubban, on the south side of the wady leading to Santa Hanneh, are probably the dwellings of the Horites," the ancient inhabitants of Idumea Proper. The pits or cavities in rocks were also sometimes used as prisons (Isaiah 24:22; 51:14; Zechariah 9:11). Those which had niches in their sides were occupied as burying-places (Ezekiel 32:23; John 11:38)."
(Easton's Bible Dictionary)

As we can see, caves were used for the following:
1. as tombs. The Jews typically buried their dead in caves.
2. as places of refuge. David hid from Saul in the cave at Adullam. Elijah hid from Jezebel in a cave. The five kings of the Amorites ran from Joshua and hid themselves in a cave.
3. as prisons. "And they shall be gathered together, as prisoners are gathered in the pit, and shall be shut up in the prison, and after many days shall they be visited" (Isaiah 24:22). The word *pit* here references a cave.
4. as temporary dwelling places. Lot and his daughters lived in a cave.

Let's establish one fact before we move forward. A creative is either a prophet or the creative is prophetic. Prophets and prophetic people reveal the heart of God to His people. This means they are lights in the darkness; they are the eyes and ears of the body of Christ. Prophets and prophetic types are gifts, even when they are burdened with the task of warning and/or judging God's people. Hebrews 12:6 reminds us this way, "For whom the Lord loves he chastens, and whips every son whom he receives." The reason this is important to note is because God will use a cave as a temporary dwelling place for a gift, but that same dwelling place has the potential to become a place of refuge (fear), a prison and eventually a tomb if the gift stays there beyond his or her season.

Caves generally have three zones. They are:
1. The entrance zone
2. The twilight zone
3. The dark zone

The entrance zone is self explanatory; it is the entrance of the cave. The twilight zone is further off into the cave, but it's still close enough to the entrance to receive some light. The dark zone is the deepest part of the cave. In this zone, there is no light.

Additionally, caves house some of the strangest creatures on the planet, but these creatures fall into three categories. They are:
- Trogloxenes:
- Troglophiles
- Troglobites

These creatures live in different parts of the cave.

Entrance	Twilight	Dark
Trogloxene	Troglophile	Troglobite
Green vegetation	Little to no plant life	No plant life

Trogloxene
1. An organism found only occasionally in caves or subterranean passages.

2. A cave guest; an animal that spends occasionally short periods in dark caves.
3. Sometimes used to characterize organisms that do not complete all of their life cycles in caves.

(Source: English Word Information/ Word Info/ 2189)

A few examples of Trogloxenes include bears, raccoon, owls and salamanders.

Troglophile

"Any animal attracted to and frequently found in underground caves or subterranean passages, but not necessarily confined to them: Some creatures are found mainly near entrances to caves and still have eyes and pigments, so they are classified as *troglophiles*."
(Source: English Word Information/ Word Info/ 2189)

Animals that live in this part of the cave include beetles, spiders, bats, worms and moths. In this section of the cave, there is little to no vegetation, and the temperature often fluctuates.

Troglobite

"A creature which lives entirely in the dark parts of underground enclosures: Troglobites are cave-dwelling creatures that navigate without eyes, go for weeks or months without food, and are believed to be able to exist for more than a hundred years."
(Source: English Word Information/ Word Info/ 2189)

Some examples of troglobites include snails, spiders, beetles, pseudoscorpions, etc. Again, these creatures have evolved into the eyeless monsters they are today.

Science has a freaky way of giving us insight into the realm of the spirit. The trogloxene is a cave guest. In other words, it does not live in a cave, but will spend a short period of time in one. If we could categorize prophets or prophetic people under these three categories, I would venture out to tell you that the trogloxene category would be the one to best describe prophets and prophetic types who were sent into caves by God. The cave for them is just a visiting place, not a dwelling place.

The prophetic introvert would be classified as a troglophile, since introverts are attracted to caves. One interesting fact to note is the trogloxene stays near the entrance, the troglophile doesn't venture too far from the entrance, but will go further than the trogloxene and the troglobite lives in the depths of caves.

Troglobites have no eyes to see. Scientists believe that this is because the cave eliminates their need for eyesight. These creatures have been in the darkness for so long that they could not survive in the light (reminiscent of demons). Of course, these creatures live in the darkest part of caves. They are blind for two reasons:
1. They've been in caves for so long that they have evolved. God placed a survival mechanism in all of mankind called adaptation. This allows most living creatures to adapt to climates and environments that would have ordinarily killed them.
2. They live in the darkest parts of caves. This is because light would kill them.

The prophet or prophetic individual who hid himself or herself in a cave or stayed there for too long would be classified as a troglobite. In other words, the prophet can live in a cave for so long that everything and everyone begins to look dark to him. To that prophet, everyone is a witch, a Jezebel, a false prophet or a false teacher. A prophet's strength is in his or her ability to see in the realm of the spirit and to hear God, but if a prophet goes too deep in the realm of the spirit and stays there for too long, he or she runs the risk of becoming dark and spooky.

You are a gift, but you don't have the luxury of giving yourself away. Anytime God's people give themselves to the wrong relationships, the wrong ideas, the wrong concepts, or the wrong careers, they bury themselves in the twilight zones of caves. And while they can escape their dingy realities, if they stay there too long, they run the risk of becoming too familiar with the cave's layout. Over time, they may find themselves venturing into the darkest part of their cave experiences.

A creative's mind has the potential to become his or her cave. Remember, there are three dimensions of the mind, according to Sigmund Freud's theory. They are:
1. conscious mind
2. subconscious mind
3. unconscious mind

Each level of the mind can be compared with the zones of a cave. Let's revisit the chart.

Entrance	Twilight	Dark
Trogloxene	Troglophile	Troglobite
Green vegetation	Little to no plant life	No plant life
Conscious Mind	Preconcious aka Subconscious Mind	Unconscious Mind

Let's get a better understanding of Freud's theory in relation to the dimensions of the mind.

The following was taken from Very Well Mind's website:
The conscious mind contains all of the thoughts, memories, feelings, and wishes of which we are aware of at any given moment. This is the aspect of our mental processing that we can think and talk about rationally. This also includes our memory, which is not always part of consciousness but can be retrieved easily and brought into awareness.
The preconscious (also known as subconscious) consists of anything that could potentially be brought into the conscious mind.
The unconscious mind is a reservoir of feelings, thoughts, urges, and memories that outside of our conscious awareness. Most of the contents of the unconscious are unacceptable or unpleasant, such as feelings of pain, anxiety, or conflict.

Freud likened the three levels of mind to an iceberg. The top of the iceberg that you can see above the water represents the conscious mind. The part of the iceberg that is submerged below the water but is still visible is the preconscious. The bulk of the iceberg that lies unseen beneath the waterline represents the unconscious."
(Source: Very Well Mind/ The Structure of the Mind, According to Freud/ Kendra Cherry)

Have you ever heard the phrase "deep in thought"? Sure, you have! It means to be so engaged or distracted by your thoughts that you become partially aware of what's going on around you. It is possible for you to "get lost in your thoughts." In the United States alone, there are 12,000 mental hospitals, and of that number, 668 of these establishments identify themselves as psychiatric hospitals (asylums). There are plenty of people in these facilities who got lost in their thoughts! They ventured off so deep into the caves of their thinking that they lost their ability to see things, people and life in general the way they used to see them. Hear me—there is absolutely nothing wrong with meditating, but the question is, what are you meditating on? The Bible tells us to meditate on the Word of God, but there are many prophets and prophetic types who meditate on conspiracy theories, numerology and just about everything they can think of. They do this because they don't know how to explain the events they've been through or the things they've seen. Consequentially, they started looking for answers in the darkness. They surrounded themselves with dark people, went to dark events, joined dark churches and became overly fascinated with dark theories. Before long, they found themselves in the trenches of their imaginations with no one to help them out, after all, they've surrounded themselves with blind people. Mark 15:14 reads, "Let them alone: they be blind leaders of the blind. And if the blind lead the blind, both shall fall into the ditch."

This is the reason community is important, and not a dark, spooky community, but a community of God-fearing believers who live above the surface—people who aren't trying to be super deep. Get this—it's okay to be deep. Just don't go too far. Don't overthink everything. Don't see the spirit realm like a matrix that you have to decode, and stop trying to figure God out. All you need is a relationship with Him. He won't make you fish for His presence. He only desires that you seek Him. You do this through prayer, fasting, communion, worship, and corporate gatherings. You also do this by reading, studying and meditating on the Word of God often.

The million dollar question I often get is, "How do I know when God is drawing me to Himself, versus when I'm withdrawing myself?" Look at the cave zones to get a better understanding. When God draws you to Himself, you'll know it's Him because He won't take you into the darkness, after all, He is the light of the world! In other words, He will draw you so that He can spend time with you, not so you can spend time by yourself! Additionally, this is the reason it's important to be planted in a good church home. God doesn't draw people out of their churches unless, of course, they are seated under a Saul or someone who is not submitted to Him. Instead, God draws religion out of people!

Let's revisit the quotes from Dr. Myles Munroe and Les Brown one more time, but this time, we're going to replace the words *grave, graveyard* and *cemetery* with the word *mind*.

"The wealthiest place on the planet is just down the road. It is the *mind*. There lie buried companies that were never started, inventions that were never made, bestselling books that were never written, and masterpieces that were never painted. In the *mind* is buried the greatest treasure of untapped potential."
– Dr. Myles Munroe (revised)

"The *mind* is the richest place on Earth, because it is here that you will find all the hopes and dreams that were never fulfilled, the books that were never written, the songs that were never sung, the inventions that were never shared, the cures that were never discovered, all because someone was too afraid to take that first step, keep with the problem, or determined to carry out their dream."
– Les Brown (revised)

Because there is still breath in your body, you don't have to bury your talents. You aren't just a gift, God has filled you up with gifts! And get this, you don't have to solve a bunch of mysteries, decode a bunch of numbers, decrypt a bunch of passwords or untangle a bunch of wires to unlock your potential. We've got to stop over-complicating God, because in our attempts to figure Him out, we are making Him look like an impossible God to unbelievers. Go into your cave if God calls you there, but don't go too deep and don't stay too long! Lastly, be accountable with your thought life. I think we can all agree that we wouldn't have 12,000 mental hospitals in America if everyone had a pastor and was submitted to their pastors.

The cave was never designed to be a tomb for the prophet; God only uses the cave as a womb and a developmental center.

> See The Purpose of Caves Diagram (Page 249)

THE CHURCH AND THE GIFT

"And God blessed them: and God said unto them, Be fruitful, and multiply, and replenish the Earth, and subdue it; and have dominion over the fish of the sea, and over the birds of the Heavens, and over every living thing that moveth upon the Earth."

Genesis 1:28

Have you ever wondered why the church, as a body, hasn't progressed much over the last few centuries or decades? Of course, we can say that the reason today's church looks so different than the churches in the forties and fifties is because of advances in modern technology. Nevertheless, while technology plays a huge role in the refacing of the church, the real reason is obvious—the world kept advancing. Their music is mastered, their productions are sharper and their delivery is more innovative. Howbeit, the church had been held captive by religious ideology, and it was considered almost sacrilegious to even attempt to make any changes. So, the church kept singing hymns and following a thousand year old model, while the youth in the church felt constricted and frustrated. Many of them were creative, innovative thinkers who were acclimated with modern technology. They passionately wanted to worship God with their creativity, but there was no platform for this in the former church model. There was no room for their gifts, unless they could sing, play the piano or praise dance. For this reason, many of the churches started looking like retirement homes—they were filled with the seasoned saints who loved the old model, but the youth found themselves going up the wrong side of the mountains of influence, looking for a way to express their creativity. Of course, this is because the world embraced their gifts and made room for them. For this reason, the turnover rate of the church is high. Needless to say, God is now raising up creative thinkers—He is now raising up leaders who understand the gifts He's placed in His children, and we now see a new wave of churches embracing gifts that had once been rejected. The leadership of the church is now being turned over, and while there still seems to be a rift between the generals and the millennials, the truth is, both are needed to continue building the structure that God has graced us to build. For this reason, God has opened the hearts and minds of many of the generals of the faith, and we are starting to see an explosion of creativity in many churches. All the same, He has humbled many of the millennials so that we can exercise our gifts in a way that gives Him glory. Amazingly enough, since this turnover started, we are even seeing some of the seasoned saints coming out of their caves, showcasing some of the most amazing displays of creativity.

In order for us to see revival, the church must turn. Sure, we've already started this rotation, however, there are still a lot of churches holding onto the old model at the expense of losing the youth. Before we go any further, let's define the word *turn*. To turn means to navigate a change of direction. Merriam-Webster defines the word *turn* this way:
to cause to move around an axis or a center: make rotate or revolve
- ◆ to execute or perform by rotating or revolving
- ◆ to cause to move around a center so as to show another side of
- ◆ to dig or plow so as to bring the lower soil to the surface

(Source: Merriam-Webster)

The Church and the Gift

Let's take a garden, for example. In order for it to become fruitful, the farmer must cultivate the soil. The word *cultivate* means to prepare. In this process, the cultivator must loosen or break up the dirt in a garden. One way to cultivate a garden is through a process called tilling. To till the ground, the farmer must use a machine called a tiller. In short, a tiller has blades attached to a metal machine. The machine is pushed or pulled by wheels. When the tiller is pushed or pulled, the blades begin to plow the ground, breaking up the fallible soil. The obvious question is, why do farmers feel the need to till the soil? This is because the soil on the surface has been exposed to moisture, air and other natural elements, all of which have caused the surface of the soil to harden. When the surface of the soil hardens, it's harder for water to penetrate the ground, and it's hard for plants underneath the soul to emerge. Tilling the soil causes the soft soil underneath to shift to the top. It also breaks up the hard soil at the surface, causing it to mix with the softer soil underneath, thus, allowing water to easily penetrate the ground. This also creates what we call fertile ground. "....and others fell upon the good ground, and yielded fruit, some a hundredfold, some sixty, some thirty" (Matthew 13:8).

The type of tiller needed is determined by the size of the garden and the depth needed to grow a specific kind of crop. For example, a small garden tiller can be used manually, but it doesn't cover much ground. Additionally, a small garden tiller must be pushed. A large tiller, also known as a plough, has blades that are both long and wide. The blades are also sharper than the ones on a traditional garden tiller. They also go deeper into the ground, plus, they cover a lot more ground than a traditional tiller. Lastly, these tillers are too heavy to push, so they are often attached to tractors and pulled, meaning, they not only cover more ground, but they are able to do this in a shorter amount of time.

The Church and the Gift

How do we apply this revelation to the church?
- ◆ Leaders must differentiate between the amount of ground they are called to cover versus the amount of ground that they can effectively cover at any given moment. For example, a man may have a vision to have and run a large farm, and that's all well and good, but if he only has a small tiller, he has to first learn to cover a small amount of ground. Trying to cover too much ground using the wrong tools will always wear out the cultivator.
- ◆ Revival is built on the backs of sons. Sure, God told Noah to build an ark, but he couldn't have done this by himself. Noah's sons helped their father to build the structure that we know as Noah's ark today. In other words, sons represent the length, width and depth of the cultivator. If a leader tries to build a large structure with very few sons, that leader will burn out his or her team. If a leader tries to build a small structure with a lot of sons, the leader will create an environment of hostility, competition and confusion. In other words, each church body has to utilize the tools available to them at any given time to accomplish God's work on the Earth.
- ◆ Every plant has to be planted at a specific depth. For example, carrots must be planted at depths of one fourth of an inch, while pumpkins require one full inch in depth to germinate. If you plant a seed too deep into the soil, you'll bury it. If you don't cover the seed with the amount of soil it needs to germinate, you expose it.
- ◆ While the leaders at the forefront have been instrumental in getting us to where we are right now, many of them have had to develop what we call thick skin. This is because they've seen, experienced and witnessed a lot. However, we still need to take advantage of modern technology and the innovative

The Church and the Gift

thinking of the new generation. This doesn't mean that the older leaders need to forfeit their platforms, after all, they have the wisdom, the experience and the boldness that we need to push forward. This does mean that each generation needs to work together so that we can dominate the mountains of influence.

God has been cultivating the ground for revival for some time now. For example:
- ◆ In the 1940's and 50's, we saw the grace of the healing anointing hit the church.
- ◆ In the 60's, we saw the gift of the evangelist return.
- ◆ In the 70's, we saw a restoration of the healing anointing.
- ◆ In the 80's, we saw the restoration of the pastor.
- ◆ In the 90's, God restored the office, the function and the anointing of the prophet.
- ◆ In the early 2000's, we began to see God reestablish the office, anointing and function of the Apostle.

What we are witnessing is God tilling the ground for revival, but for this to happen, we need tillers or cultivators that work! A tiller that does not advance the Kingdom runs the risk of becoming an antique. Understand that relevancy has a life span. In order for the church to remain relevant, we must turn the corner. If we don't want to lose a generation or squander revival, the church has to keep turning. In other words, we need cultivators to come forth who will not just push the people, but pull or lead them to the next move of God. The church must realize three things to remain relevant:
- ◆ preachers won't lead the church anymore, brains will
- ◆ we have been great at getting people saved and equipping them to work in the church, but we have not equipped them dimensionally
- ◆ we have to turn the corner on our assignment— our

> assignment is no longer to have good church, but to bring solutions

In other words, the church has to turn. Let's look a little more at the word *turn*.

Theologically, the word *turn* means to repent, to look again, to renovate one's thinking patterns or to adjust one's perspective. The Earth rotates or turns on its axis and is tilted at an angle of 23.5 degrees relative to our orbital plane which, of course, is our planet's orbit around the sun. This tilt of the axis is referred to as *obliquity* by scientists. The following information was taken from www.obliquity.com:
"Obliquity is an astronomical term describing the angle of tilt of the Earth's axis of rotation. In technical jargon, it is the angle between the plane of the Earth's equator and the plane of the Earth's orbit around the Sun.
The obliquity is approximately 23°27' but it is not fixed. Instead, it varies slowly because both the Earth's axis of rotation and its orbital motion are affected by the gravitational attractions of the Moon and planets.

No obliquity, no seasons!
If the obliquity was equal to zero, the Sun would rise at 6 a.m. and set at 6 p.m. every day of the year, everywhere in the world. There would be no long summer days and long winter nights. The Sun wouldn't be high in the sky in summer and low in winter. It would take the same path across the sky every day of the year."

In other words, the Earth has to turn in order for life to be sustained! The Earth must turn if we are to have seasons, and of course, we need seasons in order for things to grow. Each season prepares the ground for the next—every season prepares the ground for harvest. The church has to turn in order for it to grow, remain relevant and eventually dominate the seven mountains of influence. This is why God has always looked for men and women who could turn on command. A man or woman who refuses to turn is biblically referred to as stiff-necked. This word simply means that the person is prideful, haughty and stubborn.

God creates through turns. For example, the Earth turns on its axis. When a man's heart turns, this is called repentance. When God turns, this is called revelation. The turns in life aren't there to make us dizzy; instead, they are put in place to direct us towards our destinies! God moves gifts in three ways. They are: *turn* (as in gears turning), *turnaround* and *turnover*.

- The word *turn* means to change or to move something to a different position. Think of it this way—in order for gears to repeatedly turn, they need oil. This keeps the gears from rusting, becoming stuck or becoming brittle. All the same, we need the oil or, better yet, the anointing of God to help us move up the mountains of influence. Any gears that move without oil, especially at a high rate, will ignite a spark, and where there's a spark, there will soon be fire. This sounds well and good, but an ignited gift that has no oil has nothing to burn but bridges!
- The word *turnover* means to flip or rotate. It also means the rate in which employees leave a company or congregants leave a church. In order for us, as a church, to lower our turnover rate, we must turn! A turn will eventually become a cycle if it is continuously repeated. God moves us by impressing His will on our hearts. If we follow through and obey Him, we will then experience what we call a turnaround.
- Finally, there is *turnaround*. Google defines the word *turnaround* this way:

    (1). an abrupt or unexpected change, especially one that results in a more favorable situation.

(2). the process of completing or the time needed to complete a task, especially one involving receiving something, processing it, and sending it out again.

Creative gifts must master the turns or the cycles of life, but in order for this to happen, the church must make room for them! Merriam-Webster defines the word *cycle* this way:
- an interval of time during which a sequence of a recurring succession of events or phenomena is completed
- a course or series of events or operations that recur regularly and usually lead back to the starting point
- a long period of time

When we establish good cycles, Heaven and Earth both come into agreement, thus provoking Heaven to release the blessings of God into the realm of the Earth. However, when we establish bad habits, we provoke bad cycles that cause us to fall out of agreement with God. In other words, we align ourselves with the kingdom of darkness. This is when we begin to experience famines, droughts and the like. We will always experience or be subjected to the will (desires, plans) of the one running the kingdom that we're submitted to.

Cycles are oftentimes considered demonic by the church, but everything we do progresses through circular stages of upward development. Simply put, growth is the same cycle on another level. Below are a few examples of cycles that we all endure:
1. Biological Cycles
2. Emotional Cycles
3. Chemical Cycles
4. Financial Cycles
5. Revelational Cycles
6. Inspirational Cycles

7. Social Cycles
8. Educational Cycles
9. Intercessory Cycles
10. Productivity Cycles
11. Sleep Cycles
12. Gift Cycles

Again, God has always looked for men who could turn—men who were not enslaved by their own ideologies or by religion. When He finds or raises them up, they become pioneers of change—men and women who take the worship of God to another level.

We all know that God has given the gift of five-fold leaders to the church, however, He has also given us the gift of creatives, and some of these creatives aren't gracing the pulpits; they are in the pews, trying to figure how to silence the sound of their potential. This is the reason there should be a connection between the pulpit and the pews—one that would allow the creative to use his or her gifts in the church. The point is, the church has rejected God's gifts for far too long. We, as a church, can't keep rejecting every wave of God that hits! We have to embrace God's gifts if we want to remain relevant.

CLIFFS AND CAVES

The Lord wants to give us understanding in three areas:
- ◆ boundaries
- ◆ breaking points
- ◆ back stages

How do you deal with boundaries? First and foremost, what is a boundary? Merriam-Webster defines boundary this way, "something that indicates or fixes a limit or extent." Another word for *boundary* is *rule*. Let's look at Isaiah 53:19, which reads, "So shall they fear the name of the LORD from the west, and his glory from the rising of the sun. When the enemy shall come in like a flood, the Spirit of the LORD shall lift up a standard against him." In this scripture, we see the word *standard*. This word means a measure of rule or a boundary. In other words, God will only allow the enemy to go "so far." We see an example of this in the book of Job, when the Lord gave Satan permission to test Job. Job 2:6 reads, "And Jehovah said unto Satan, Behold, he is in thy hand; only spare his life." Satan was not allowed to kill Job; this was his standard or his measure of rule.

"And the LORD God took the man, and put him into the garden of Eden to dress it and to keep it. And the LORD God commanded the man, saying, Of every tree of the garden you may freely eat: But of the tree of the knowledge of good and evil, you shall not eat of it: for in the day that you eat thereof you shall surely die."
Genesis 2:15-17

Cliffs and Caves

"Now the serpent was more subtle than any beast of the field which the LORD God had made. And he said to the woman, Yes, has God said, You shall not eat of every tree of the garden? And the woman said to the serpent, We may eat of the fruit of the trees of the garden: But of the fruit of the tree which is in the middle of the garden, God has said, You shall not eat of it, neither shall you touch it, lest you die. And the serpent said to the woman, You shall not surely die: For God does know that in the day you eat thereof, then your eyes shall be opened, and you shall be as gods, knowing good and evil. And when the woman saw that the tree was good for food, and that it was pleasant to the eyes, and a tree to be desired to make one wise, she took of the fruit thereof, and did eat, and gave also to her husband with her; and he did eat. And the eyes of them both were opened, and they knew that they were naked; and they sewed fig leaves together, and made themselves aprons."

Genesis 3:1-7

What we see in the above scriptures is God setting boundaries, and then Satan tempting Eve to cross those boundaries. She fell into this temptation, and from there, she tempted her husband to do the same. Of course, he fell into the demonic snare as well, and this was the fall of mankind. Mankind fell because the couple "went too far." Mankind fell because neither Adam nor Eve respected the boundaries that God had put in place to protect them. Anytime a boundary is crossed, the person who crossed it is guilty of the crime of trespassing.

Your success will always be determined by how you respect boundaries. At any given time, you may feel as if you are at your breaking point, but if you are ever going to grow (mature), you will have cross the chasm of comfort—you will have to leave your comfort zone and enter into convenience. The membrane between your comfort zone and convenience is very turbulent; it's a place of transition. Most people die in the place of transition; they die trying to get through the process of transitioning. If the children of Israel would have stayed in Egypt, they would have been okay. Nevertheless, they wanted their freedom, and because they complained in the midst of their transition, they died in the in-between, in the process, in the turbulence of their transition. If you really want something better, if you really want something new, if you really want something stronger, if you really want God to do something in your life, you have to be willing to risk it all. You can't leave where you are and think you're going to get to the promise without coming across the Philistines in the wilderness. You can't leave where you are and think you're going to get to the promise without the Amalekites coming against you in the wilderness. There's going to be a lot of enemies between your promise and the promise manifested; there's going to be a lot of enemies between the prophesy and the promise. There's going to be a lot of persecution in between both worlds, and you must be willing to endure it. This is what the Bible calls long-suffering. Long suffering has two legs; they are patience and perseverance. Without one, the other cannot stand for too long. This is also why God said in Galatians 6:9, "And let us not be weary in well-doing: for in due season we shall reap, if we faint not."

I earned my degree in theater, and one of the biggest challenges in theater is waiting on your turn. As the play is going on, you are sitting on the sideline waiting for your turn. You have to stay attentive—you have to watch the play. You cannot get distracted, because if you miss your cue, you will miss your moment. Of course, this would offset the rhythm of the entire show. You absolutely have to be in place, waiting on your turn. You can't come out too early and you can't come out too late. You have to be right on time, right on schedule. Guess what? This is what the Lord

Cliffs and Caves

has been doing *in* you, and this is what the Lord has been doing *with* you. He slowed you down in some seasons and He sped you up in others. This is because He's trying to syncopate you to the pace of your purpose so that you will arrive in your promised land right on time. For this reason, He has to slow you down when you're going too fast, and He has to speed you up when you're going too slow. Think of it this way. The Earth spins at one thousand miles an hour. If it were to slow down or speed up, every living thing on Earth would be affected. The following information was taken from Popular Science's website:

"Centrifugal force from the Earth's spin is constantly trying to fling you off the planet, sort of like a kid on the edge of a fast merry-go-round. For now, gravity is stronger and it keeps you grounded. But if Earth were to spin faster, the centrifugal force would get a boost, says NASA astronomer Sten Odenwald.

Currently, if you weigh about 150 pounds in the Arctic Circle, you might weigh 149 pounds at the equator. That's because of the extra centrifugal force that's generated as the equator spins faster combats gravity. Press fast-forward on that, and your weight would drop even further.

Odenwald calculates that eventually, if the equator revved up to 17,641 mph, the centrifugal force would be great enough that you would be essentially weightless."
(Source: Popular Science/ What Would Happen if the Earth Started to Spin Faster/Sarah Fecht)

The site went on to report that if our days would become shorter, we'd suffer from constant jet lag, we'd see stronger hurricanes and so on. The point is, if God has the Earth spinning at a specific rate—please understand that He's moving you at a specific speed as well. The prodigal son wanted to get his inheritance before his father died, and because he wasn't mature enough to manage it, he squandered it. After he'd lost everything, humility met him where he stood, and he'd gone into a cave of sorts. Luke 15:17-19 reads, "But when he came to himself he said, How many hired servants of my father's have bread enough and to spare, and I perish here with hunger! I will arise and go to my father, and will say unto him, Father, I have sinned against heaven, and in thy sight: I am no more worthy to be called your son: make me as one of thy hired servants."

While he had not gone into a physical cave, the prodigal son had gone into a mental cave. This is a time of reflection, reevaluation and repentance. This is similar to those moments when we were immature and had gotten a large sum of money. Most of us went out and bought almost everything in sight. We were high in those moments; we were carefree in those moments. Nevertheless, once we'd spent more than a third of what we had, we'd gone through moments of reflection; this is where we tried to figure out where every dollar went. This is when we regretted spending so frivolously, and this is when many of us went through what is commonly referred to as buyers' remorse.

"And Lot went up out of Zoar, and dwelt in the mountain, and his two daughters with him; for he feared to dwell in Zoar: and he dwelt in a cave, he and his two daughters" (Genesis 19:30). We will not exegete this scripture, I just want to show you something in the verbiage of it. Don't worry about the historicity or the surrounding verses. We are just looking at this to get a principle. I want you to look at the juxtaposition of two phrases:
1. "he dwelt *in* the mountain, not *on* the mountain."
2. "and he dwelt in the mountain, and his two daughters with him for he feared to dwell in Zoar and he dwelt in the cave."

I want to submit to you that these two phases, albeit different, are enforcing the same principle. It's pretty much

Cliffs and Caves

saying that to dwell in a mountain means to dwell in a cave, after all, a cave is a carved-out piece of rock or a space that has been made in the side of a mountain. When we say mountains, we are talking about shapers of society. Consider the Seven Mountain Mandate. If we are going to be successful as a church, if we are going to advance the Kingdom of God, if we are going to see dominion over the Earth, if we are going to see the Spirit of God and God's culture superimposed on the culture of the world, it's going to take Christians to infiltrate, influence and then dominate the seven mountains of the world. Those mountains, once again, are Government, Media, Arts & Entertainment, Business, Family, Religion and Education. It is not our job to become real anointed; it is not our assignment to become a superstar in the church. It's our job to become anointed so that we can be sent out with apostolic authority into the marketplace, this way, we can become agents for the wealth of the wicked to be transferred into the church. We are made to rule.

On your way up the mountain or mountains that you are called to, it is important for you to understand that there are strategic seasons where you need rest. There are strategic seasons when God will hide you; there are strategic seasons where God renovates, re-engineers and restores you. These are strategic seasons of isolation and separation. Again, this season is what we call the cave.

You need to understand why the cave is important to the ecosystem of your gift, and why it is important for you to strategically take time to hide yourself. Sometimes, seasons of obscurity will be voluntary, while at other times, they will be God-initiated. There will be times when you won't understand why all your friends suddenly stopped calling you or why everybody in your life has left you. These separations aren't always permanent; sometimes, they're just

Cliffs and Caves

for a season. I have great friends, but just like everyone else, we go through cycles and we go through seasons. We will have seasons where we talk every day, all day and then, we go through seasons where we won't talk for months. It's not that their love for me has expired. No. I am dealing with the cave. I'm working out my own soul's salvation with fear and trembling. I'm allowing God to process me for the next page and stage of my life. There will be times when you are silent and you won't have anything to say—there will be times when God will supernaturally shut down your tongue so that you don't rewrite the past.

"And Jesus, when he was baptized, went up straightway out of the water: and, lo, the heavens were opened unto him, and he saw the Spirit of God descending like a dove, and lighting upon him: And lo a voice from heaven, saying, This is my beloved Son, in whom I am well pleased."
Matthew 3:16

Jesus had just been baptized. He'd just been anointed. In modern terms, He'd just been licensed and ordained. He'd just been released into ministry, and His first act wasn't to preach a revival. Instead, He went through a process of training and He passed the test. Not only was He licensed by God and ordained by Heaven, He was anointed in front of a congregation of believers and unbelievers who'd come together to see John, the Baptist. The Lord submitted to the baptism, and when He came up out of the water, the heavens opened and everybody heard thunder and saw lightning. God said, "This is my beloved Son in whom I am well pleased." He affirmed Jesus in front of everybody. You would think that this would be enough. Most of us would have reasoned this way— "I'm anointed, I'm affirmed, I got my papers, so I'm good. Let me go get me a nice website, an Instagram page, and a Facebook page. Let start doing Facebook Live; let me launch my ministry." Nevertheless,

Jesus said, "No!" Yes, you are anointed, but the next stage of your development is the wilderness. Many people ask, "When do I get to use my anointing?" The answer is simple. You are going to use your anointing in your season of temptation; this is before you can use it in ministry. You are not anointed to perform before people. The first time you release your anointing should be when you're utilizing it to break your own perversion! Your anointing has to break your issues off of you before it can set anyone else free. Matthew 7:5 says it this way, "Thou hypocrite, cast out first the beam out of thine own eye; and then shalt thou see clearly to cast out the mote out of thy brother's eye."

God will let you test your gift, not on people, but on yourself. What if I told you that's what He is waiting for? If you are still dealing with the vacillation of your emotional stability, and you still can't get up out the bed because of depression, it is clear that your gift doesn't yet work on you. Why would God trust you to help someone else and pull them out of depression when you can't pull yourself out? David said, "I had to encourage myself in the Lord." This means that, at some point, David was depressed, but he couldn't keep looking for somebody else to encourage him, so he found his lyre and started playing until he'd encouraged himself. When he found the right key, when he found the right rhythm, and when he found the right melody, his praise became a weapon for him. After that, every time that spirit of heaviness would come his way, he knew how to address it. He said, "He teaches my hands to war, so that a bow of steel is broken by my arms" (Psalm 18:34). Because of this, God give him mastery over his gift, meaning, he could lift depression off of others. His gift turned into a weapon because of mastery.

After Jesus was anointed, He went into the wilderness. From there, He was tempted with three temptations, each one of them were incrementally heavier than the first. Each test, each trial, each temptation increased in strength as Jesus went up. Then was Jesus led up of the Spirit to be tempted. Nevertheless, the Bible is clear that God will not tempt you beyond what you can handle or bear. Notice the Spirit of God led Jesus into an uncomfortable and inconvenient situation knowing that it's going to challenge Him or grow Him. Matthew 4:2 says, "And when had fasted for forty days and forty nights He was afterwards hungry," so He was hungry. This is when the tempter came! Notice the tempter only comes when you are hungry. This is why one of the ways you silence the devil is through satisfaction. You see, the devil can't talk to you in an area that you are satisfied. This is why Apostle Paul said, "I know how be abased and I know how to abound." I know how to have a lot and I know how to have a little. I'm not going to allow what I have to make me disgruntled or to make me bitter. This is because my place of bitterness has the potential to become a place where the enemy can dwell.

Notice that the first temptation Jesus had to deal with was fleshly, carnal or base-level stuff. How do you deal with your own perversion and your own proclivities? How do you deal with your own problems? Remember, Jesus had to learn how to deal with His stuff before God gave Him authority over somebody else's stuff. So, the first level of temptation is your own stuff. You don't qualify to help other people with their stuff until you've learned how to handle your own issues. How can you look at someone else and see the tree in their eye, when you can't see the entire forest in your own?

Next, let's look at Matthew 4:4. "But he answered and said, It is written, Man shall not live by bread alone, but by every word that proceedeth out of the mouth of God." Jesus dealt with that temptation by refusing to use His authority or power to gratify Himself. He refused to waste a miracle trying to solidify His self-worth.

"Then the devil taketh him into the holy city; and he set him on the pinnacle of the temple, and saith unto him, If thou art the Son of God, cast thyself down: for it is written, He shall give his angels charge concerning thee: and, on their hands they shall bear thee up, lest haply thou dash thy foot against a stone" (Matthew 4:5-6). As you can see, at first, He was dealing with ground level stuff, but now, He found Himself at the pinnacle of the temple; this is the height of the religious system. This is the top of the Mountain of Religion. You can see the incremental increase. The enemy took Him up to the steeple of the highest mountain (the Mountain of Religion) and tempted Him there. Height speaks of rank. He was at the top, but He was also on the edge. This is when the devil said, "Cast thou self down." What he was saying is, "Take your own life." In other words, you are not the only one who has thought about committing suicide. Every great man and woman who has dealt with the pressures of expectation has considered throwing in the towel—mental, emotionally, and sometimes, even physically. Thoughts of suicide are a few temptations that you must go through and get past if you are ever going to be great. This is why you have to encourage yourself like Job did and say, "Though he slay me, yet will I trust in him!" Remember, Psalm 20:7; it reads, "Some trust in chariots, and some in horses: but we will remember the name of the LORD our God."

Again, Satan told Jesus to cast Himself down. Hear me—Satan doesn't mind you knowing that you are anointed, and he doesn't mind you having a title if you are still struggling with depression. What good is it to be gifted if you can't help anyone with your gift because of your emotional and mental instability? We all go through it. It's a human thing to deal with thoughts of suicide. Don't think that you are an anomaly; Jesus dealt with it. Elijah, at one point, said, "Lord kill me." This was the man who'd called fire down from Heaven—the one who'd killed the prophets of Baal—the one who'd opened up the heavens and caused it rained again. This was the one who'd raised the dead. Elijah had performed seven miracles, and yet, he wanted to commit suicide. Most people have done a single miracle, howbeit, they are ready to kill themselves!

Jesus answered the devil with, "Thou should not tempt the Lord your God." Matthew 4:8 says, "Again, the devil taketh him unto an exceeding high mountain, and showeth him all the kingdoms of the world, and the glory of them; and he said unto him, all these things will I give thee, if thou wilt fall down and worship me." Earlier, we read a verse that told us that Lot had gone inside of a mountain with his daughters. It then went on to say that they'd dwelt in a cave, meaning the inside of a mountain and a cave are one and the same. Matthew 4:8 said that Jesus had gone into an exceedingly high mountain. What I'm trying to deduce is that Jesus had gone into a cave. Even Jesus had to deal with cave seasons; He had to endure the seasons of silence, seasons of isolation and seasons where He felt forgotten and overlooked. He was still anointed, but He was overlooked. He was still anointed, but nobody knew Him. He was still anointed, but nobody was listening to Him. The only thing that He could hear was the sound of His own voice, after all, He was in a cave. He was in darkness. From there, He had to learn how to deal with three things:
1. He had to learn how to deal with boundaries.
2. He had to learn how to deal with breaking points.
3. He had to learn how to deal with back stages.

The Destiny Diagram™ describes how we all start out as a dot; that dot represents you. One of the reasons you are represented as a dot is because I want you to understand how small you are to the purpose of God. When it comes to you accomplishing the will of God for your life, your desire, your will and your self-image are very small. Let's look at 1 Samuel 15:17, which reads, "And Samuel said, Though thou wast little in thine own sight, wast thou not made the head of the tribes of Israel? And Jehovah anointed thee king over Israel." He said that when Saul was small in his own eyes, he obeyed God. This is because when we don't see ourselves as much, we depend on God. Nevertheless, when Saul became big in his own eyes, he began to disobey God or feel as if he had the right to debate or deliberate with God's Word or God's opinion. One of the things that get people in trouble is when they start believing their own hype. This is when they fall in love with other people's opinions of them. It's amazing how people believe the compliments, but they often reject constructive criticism. Don't get drunk off any of it.

Also, on the Destiny Diagram™, you'll see time, which is linear. It has a beginning, a middle and an end. This is your lifespan. Your giftings are located on here as well. You can also call this purpose. The Destiny Diagram™ also deals with your calling, maturity and character (fruits). In order for us to accomplish our purpose, it is very important that we all understand that we have the same purpose. Our purpose is to defeat and to destroy the works of the enemy. 1 John 3:8 says, "For this purpose the Son of God was manifested, that he might destroy the works of the devil." Please understand that the sons of God became the sons of men so that the sons of men could become the sons of God. The reason Jesus came to Earth was to die; He came to shed His blood so that by His blood, we would have the ability to become sons of God. Why is this important? Because the reason you are being made or manifested as a son of God is because a son of God is a true representative or reflection of God. This is someone who is sensitive to His will and someone who is obedient to His Word. The reason God wants to make you a son is because He wants to grow you up into the admonition of the Lord until you are the full stature of the measure of Christ, according to Ephesians 4. The reason God wants to grow you into a mature Christian or into a son of God is because, when you become mature, you have the ability to defeat the works of the devil. This means that if there's poverty in your life, when grow up in your anointing, you will realize and recognize your assignment in the Kingdom of God. Additionally, you won't continue to allow poverty to stay in your life. Instead, you will break the chains of poverty off your mind. You will stop overspending and start budgeting your money so that your children and your children's children will have a legacy. Your job, once again, is to destroy the works of the devil. The works of the devil stagnate the progression of God's Kingdom. Whenever you break one them in your life, this accelerates the advancement of God's Kingdom, not just geographically, but also dimensionally. This is not just in our lives, but also in the lives of our families. This is why you have to mature, pray, read your Bible, withstand temptation and fast. Your first journey is about getting you to become a mature believer, and after this, the second leg of your journey is all about you advancing the Kingdom of God. This is your purpose; this is also your calling. Paul said it this way, "I press towards the prize for the *high calling* of God in Christ."

Again, we don't just grow in length, we also grow in height. We don't just grow in time, we also grow in maturity. If I grow wide without growing tall, I will topple over and become a big midget in the spirit. I will have a whole bunch of information that I wouldn't be able to do anything with. I would know all the scriptures, but wouldn't be able to abide by a single one of them. It is God's will that we grow in dimensions. Character brings balance to your gifting. Height brings balance to your width. Maturity brings balance to your skill or your competence.

Every gift creates a lane. Proverbs 18:16 says, "A man's gift maketh room for him, And bringeth him before great men." Your gift is not there to pay your bills, your gift is there to bear fruit. Your gift makes room for your character. Your gift prepares the way for who you truly are. This is why your gift can get you in the room, but once you get in the room, you must have character if you're going to sustain your position. Your gifts create lanes, regardless of whether you are a doctor, a lawyer, a teacher, a pilot, an actor, a singer, a cosmetologist, a fashion designer, a painter or a fortune five hundred entrepreneur. You are not going to stay in one lane your whole life. Every lane you have ever lived in taught you lessons that will culminate into your overall maturity.

The first level of training comes through observation, meaning, you have to be able to watch or study other people do what you're called to do. Hear me—geniuses don't have time to go to lunch with you all the time, so you have to get some of your training vicariously. You have to be willing to create distance so that you can get a good view of what and where you're called to. This is why Elijah said, "If you see me when I'm taken up, you can have what's on my life." He didn't say, "If you talk to me." He said, "If you see me." So, you have lanes, of course, at some point that you have to exit. You don't live in the same lane your whole life. Not only do we live in lanes, we also live on levels—these are levels of maturity and levels of character. For example, when I was at the lower level, I could sing, but I also still used my mouth to cuss. As I started to elevate in maturity, I started learning the language of my next level. But I also had to switch lanes. I started learning how to sow, I started learning how to cook—whatever the case may be.

The Destiny Diagram™ also represents a season, a chapter

and a time. Each chapter can be made up of many different pages, a volume or a lifespan. In order for you to get to one place or another, you have to use an apparatus called the ladder. In order to reach beyond your height, it usually takes a ladder. A ladder has steps; we can call these steps of mastery or steps of skills. At the bottom of the ladder, there is the infancy level, but at the top of the ladder is the maturity level. When a man starts his journey as a husband, he doesn't start out at the top of the ladder. He starts off as a newlywed and he has to grow into the husband God created him to be. When a woman starts a new job, she has to start at the bottom of the ladder. Even if she starts at the top of an organization, she still has to start at the bottom of the information, meaning, she has to grow!

Again, Jesus is that ladder. He is the only legal apparatus that gives us the ability to go from one level to the next. Jesus said, "If any man wants to come to the Father he must come through me. If any person comes any other way, he is a thief and a robber." There's a whole bunch of people who are successful, but they've stolen their success.

Of course, the ladder can be turned. If you turn the ladder, it looks like steps. When you are climbing a ladder—when you are ascending the heart of Jesus—when you are going from ground-level temptation to mid-level temptation and then to mountaintop temptation, you have to climb. When you are climbing, you are dealing with two things: cliffs and caves. You have a cave—this is the womb of your development, and you have a cliff. The same cliff you must conquer going up can become a source of temptation going down. The same cliff you had to conquer going up, if you are not careful, can trip you up as you descend. This is what we call boundaries. As you are going up, you have to know your boundaries. If you don't know your boundaries, you will fall off the mountain. The higher you go up, the greater the fall.

If you want to be great, you will have to deal with the pressure of keeping it together every single day.

You have the cliff and you have the cave. As you are going up, the cave is there to strategically hide you from storms. As you are climbing up the mountain, the more violent the winds will become. The winds are the opinions of people and the philosophies of men. You will be tossed to and fro by every wind of doctrine until you anchor yourself in the Word of God. As you begin to increase or, in other words, the higher you go up, the stronger the winds will be. This means you have to be even more stable, both emotionally and mentally. If you are going to progress in any area, whether it's vocation, calling or whatever the case may be, you must increase. So, as you're going up, God carves out times and moments for you to rest, be restored, get some renewal, reinvent yourself, re-brand and then, you come out transformed, reinvigorated and wiser. Sometimes, it will feel like God is pulling you back. When this happens, you will notice that everyone around you seems to be going ahead of you. They are getting married before you, starting their businesses before you and releasing their books before you. Your challenge is to resist getting offended. You have to refuse to compare yourself to them and to just trust the pace that God has for you.

See Cliffs and Caves Diagram (Page 243)

THE GENESIS OF A GIFT

"And the king of Egypt spake to the Hebrew midwives, of which the name of the one was Shiphrah, and the name of the other Puah: And he said, When ye do the office of a midwife to the Hebrew women, and see them upon the stools; if it be a son, then ye shall kill him: but if it be a daughter, then she shall live. But the midwives feared God, and did not as the king of Egypt commanded them, but saved the men children alive. And the king of Egypt called for the midwives, and said unto them, Why have ye done this thing, and have saved the men children alive? And the midwives said unto Pharaoh, Because the Hebrew women are not as the Egyptian women; for they are lively, and are delivered ere the midwives come in unto them. Therefore God dealt well with the midwives: and the people multiplied, and waxed very mighty. And it came to pass, because the midwives feared God, that he made them houses. And Pharaoh charged all his people, saying, Every son that is born ye shall cast into the river, and every daughter ye shall save alive."

(Exodus 1:15-22)

The first book of Exodus details a very dark period in Jewish history. The Jews were slaves in the foreign, yet familiar, land of Egypt. Pharaoh had gone out of his way to oppress and subjugate them, but to no avail. When he discovered that his attempts to extinguish what he deemed to be a threat had been futile, he decided to take a more wicked approach. This time, he decided to kill off all the male children born to Jewish women. But what would make a human being decide to oppress and kill other humans, especially defenseless children? Answer: fear.

Fear comes on the scene when we attempt to forecast our futures on our own or through the use of a demonic medium. Matthew 6:34 instructs us to, "Take therefore no thought for the morrow: for the morrow shall take thought for the things of itself. Sufficient unto the day is the evil thereof." Anytime we consider what tomorrow has the potential to bring with it, we open the door for fear. When the spirit of fear comes on the scene, it brings two other spirits with it: control and witchcraft. In Pharaoh's case, he feared (and forecast) that if the Jews were not brought under subjection, they would eventually ally themselves with the enemies of Egypt if a war should break out. To stop what he deemed to be a credible threat, Pharaoh enacted a plan to kill off all the young males born to Jewish women. What was Pharaoh looking at? He was looking at the potential of the Jews. For this reason, God often hides the potential of a person or a people. This, of course, is to protect them while they develop their strength, just as the womb protects a baby until the baby is strong enough to live on its own.

What is potential? Gal Einai (Revealing the Torah's Inner Dimension) says the following:
> "The two letters of the full spelling of the *kaf*, are the initial letters of the two Hebrew words: *koach* ("potential") and *poel* ("actual"). Thus, the *kaf* hints at the power latent within the spiritual realm of the potential to fully manifest itself in the physical realm of the actual. God must create the world continuously; otherwise Creation would instantaneously vanish. His potential is therefore actualized at each moment. This concept is referred to as "the power to actualize potential ever-present within the actualized."

(https://www.inner.org/hebleter/kaf.htm/ The Hebrew Letters KAF)

Potential can be defined as power in its embryonic or fetal stages. It is authority locked up in the womb of a living thing. The potential of a thing can be its perceived power or its actual power. Perceived power is not actual power; it is the perception of power that has been determined by an individual or group. Actual power (in the potential stage) is latent power. It is power in development that is hidden, concealed or has not come fully to fruition. How do we respond to power, either perceived or actual? With force, of course. Force, according to physics, is anything that changes the motion of an object. Force is just power that moves contrary to another power. And of course, any power that is used in an ungodly manner is categorized as witchcraft. This is why later on in the book of Exodus, we find Pharaoh surrounded by sorcerers who were able to mimic some of the miracles that Moses did. Remember, any time the spirit of fear comes in, it brings with it the spirits of control and witchcraft.

It's safe to say that Satan fears our actual power as well our potential. He is terrified of our abilities to reproduce, not just children, but to birth out many of the same works he once watched God perform. This is because he knows his time is short, and he knows that God is going to birth out men and women who repeatedly destroy his works and wreak havoc on his kingdom. For this reason, he loves to kill babies while they are in the womb and when they are newborns. We know that he comes to steal, kill and destroy, but what we have to realize is that anytime Satan attacks a group, he knows that someone is going to come out of that group who has been empowered to bring hell to his kingdom. Hell is nothing but the kingdom of darkness on fire.

The Genesis of a Gift

One of the most interesting books in the Bible is the book of Genesis. The reason for this is because we witness so many dynamics taking place in the fifty chapters that make up this book. First, we read about God creating the Earth, and then, we get to mentally revisit the moment when God pulled everything we'd ever need out of Himself. Eventually, we are introduced to Adam, and not long after Adam takes his first steps, we are introduced to Eve. As the book continues, we are introduced to Satan, and then we witness the fall of mankind. By the time we get to the last book of Genesis, mankind has long been kicked out of the Garden of Eden and a whole new conversation is taking place. Instead, we find Joseph at the height of his assignment; we find Joseph at the peak of his potential. As a matter of fact, his potential by this time was no longer just potential. It had been actualized; it had become fruit. At the height of his potential, Joseph had been appointed by the Pharaoh of that era as his right-hand man. Pharaoh referred to Joseph as Zaphnathpaaneah, nevertheless, you'll notice that the Bible continues to reference him as Joseph. This is because a man's inheritance is locked up in his name. Joseph was the son of the man formerly known as Jacob: Israel.

"And Jacob went out from Beersheba, and went toward Haran. And he lighted upon a certain place, and tarried there all night, because the sun was set; and he took of the stones of that place, and put them for his pillows, and lay down in that place to sleep. And he dreamed, and behold a ladder set up on the Earth, and the top of it reached to Heaven: and behold the angels of God ascending and descending on it. And, behold, the LORD stood above it, and said, I am the LORD God of Abraham thy father, and the God of Isaac: the land whereon thou liest, to thee will I give it, and to thy seed; and thy seed shall be as the dust of the earth, and thou shalt spread abroad to the west, and to the east, and to the north, and to the south: and in thee and in

thy seed shall all the families of the Earth be blessed. And, behold, I am with thee, and will keep thee in all places whither thou goest, and will bring thee again into this land; for I will not leave thee, until I have done that which I have spoken to thee of. And Jacob awaked out of his sleep, and he said, Surely the LORD is in this place; and I knew it not."
Genesis 28:10-16

"And God appeared unto Jacob again, when he came out of Padanaram, and blessed him. And God said unto him, Thy name is Jacob: thy name shall not be called any more Jacob, but Israel shall be thy name: and he called his name Israel. And God said unto him, I am God Almighty: be fruitful and multiply; a nation and a company of nations shall be of thee, and kings shall come out of thy loins; and the land which I gave Abraham and Isaac, to thee I will give it, and to thy seed after thee will I give the land. And God went up from him in the place where he talked with him. And Jacob set up a pillar in the place where he talked with him, even a pillar of stone: and he poured a drink offering thereon, and he poured oil thereon. And Jacob called the name of the place where God spake with him, Bethel."
Genesis 35:9-15

By the time we get to Genesis 50, a new thing is about to take place. Joseph is about to pass away after being reconciled to his father and his brothers, and the Jews are about to find themselves in the genesis of another season, but this season is referred to as Exodus. In the beginning (or genesis) of the book of Exodus, we see that a new Pharaoh has taken the throne. This particular Pharaoh was unfamiliar with Joseph and he happened to be the homicidal maniac of his era. His genocide, however, was the oppression and enslaving of the Jews. This Pharaoh was one of the first men to execute what we now refer to as population control. Human population control is a political campaign designed to maintain or decrease the size of any given population, oftentimes through oppression, birth control, colonization, sterilization and genocides. One notable example of population control was the Holocaust (1941-1945). During the Holocaust, Nazis killed seven out of ten Jews living in Europe, which totaled out to be approximately six million Jews. Before the Holocaust, Europe's Jewish population boasted of 9.5 million Jews. Nowadays, one of the most effective, yet undetected, methods of human depopulation is called "gay marriage." Homosexuality is not just promoted by the media, it is glamorized by both Hollywood and politicians, and anyone who speaks against it is demonized. Nevertheless, it is nothing more than a romantic genocide of sorts.

Many governments have tried to control the population of their country. China, for example, had a one-child policy, whereas couples were only allowed to have one child. This policy was active for 35 years and it was relaxed in January of 2016. Chinese couples are now allowed to have two children. The one-child policy is the reason that China's female population is so dense compared to their male population. Parents would often abort, kill or abandon their newborn daughters in favor of having a male heir. In China and India alone, it is estimated that around two million female infants go missing each year. The mass murdering of infants is called infanticide. Female infanticide is common all over Asia; it is practiced in China, Nepal, South Korea and India.

Another form of infanticide is abortion. In 2015 alone, Americans had over six hundred thousand abortions. Abortions are common in the lower to lower middle-class. Guttmacher Institute reports that:
- ◆ 26% of the abortions performed in the United States were on women who were at the federal poverty

level.
- ◆ 30% of the abortions performed in the United States were on women who were below the federal poverty level.

This means that abortion tends to be centralized around and promoted to poor American women, especially minorities. This also means that we are still experiencing genocides today, but these mass murderings are labeled as choices and then promoted.

"And the children of Israel were fruitful, and increased abundantly, and multiplied, and waxed exceeding mighty; and the land was filled with them. Now there arose up a new king over Egypt, which knew not Joseph. And he said unto his people, Behold, the people of the children of Israel are more and mightier than we: Come on, let us deal wisely with them; lest they multiply, and it come to pass, that, when there falleth out any war, they join also unto our enemies, and fight against us, and so get them up out of the land. Therefore they did set over them taskmasters to afflict them with their burdens. And they built for Pharaoh treasure cities, Pithom and Raamses."

(Exodus 1:7-11)

As we can see in the book of Exodus, Pharaoh saw how fast the Jewish population was increasing and he took notice of their potential. Feeling intimidated, he decided to oppress the Jews, hoping this would kill off a large number of them and weaken the ones who remained. Instead, he found out a truth that social scientists can attest to today, and that is, oppressed people have nothing else to do but make babies. This survival mechanism is the human's instinctual response to the threat of extermination. Whenever people are oppressed, they have limited or no access to education, they have increased mortality rates and they either marry early or, in many cases, some of the fathers will die prematurely or abandon their families. Of course, when there's no father in the home, children are forced to grow up fast, which leads to a lot of young women having babies outside of the marital covenant.

"But the more they afflicted them, the more they multiplied and grew. And they were grieved because of the children of Israel."

(Exodus 1:12)

The Jews didn't just grow in number, they grew in strength. Anytime a man repeatedly uses his physical body to lift heavy things, the body responds by increasing its muscle tissue. This means that the Jewish men started looking like body builders. This intimidated Pharaoh all the more.

After Moses confronted Pharaoh and freed the Jews, they then found themselves in yet another genesis, but this time, they were in the wilderness. The wilderness represents the womb of a new season. This was a season of cycles; it was a season designed to wash away the residue of Egypt from them. Of course, we know the rest. Instead of getting delivered, the Jews could not stop complaining and reminiscing about their abusive ex: Egypt. For this reason, a journey that was designed to take eleven days ended up taking forty years.

The gestation period of a human baby is nine months. During this time, the infant must endure three seasons; science refers to these seasons as trimesters. During the first season of the embryo's life, the developing child has to endure several critical processes, including a process called implantation, which generally takes place around week four. As a matter of fact, eighty percent of miscarriages occur in the first trimester of pregnancy. This is similar to a thought, an idea or a concept attempting to implant itself in the heart of a gift, but is instead rejected and miscarried because of fear, doubt, rejection or procrastination. Nevertheless, the embryos that survive the first trimester go on to become fetuses, and the chance for miscarriage decreases significantly.

During the second trimester of pregnancy, an infant's organs become fully developed. This is the period when the mother will begin to feel the movements of her unborn baby. During this season, the mother's appetite will increase and her abdomen will begin to swell, revealing to those around her that she is expecting. This is the most comfortable period for most pregnant women, and it is during this trimester that the unborn infants can hear and recognize the voice of their mothers.

Finally, there is the third trimester. During this trimester, the baby is fully formed and can survive outside of its mother's womb. Nevertheless, just because it can survive outside of the womb doesn't mean that it is ready to be born. This is still a time of concealment, and while the womb is a dark place, it is still a place where the baby is nourished, housed and protected. This the most uncomfortable trimester for most women, given the fact that their body weight has increased significantly, they are constantly feeling the weight of the fetus on their bladders and their energy levels have decreased. To make matters worse, cruise ships and airlines typically will not allow expectant mothers who are 28 weeks or greater to board them. This can be frustrating to the expectant mother, and during this season of her pregnancy, she may feel like she's being picked on. Her doctor keeps trying to put her on bed rest and everyone who sees her insists that she sit down. She may find herself in a nesting phase, where she feels this overwhelming and instinctual urge to clean her house and rearrange the furniture in her home in preparation for the arrival of her new baby. Nevertheless, no one around her is nesting, meaning, she may feel like she's all alone in her attempt to ready her home and her family for the new arrival. In this, we find that the mother has survived the genesis of her pregnancy and is now prepping for the revelation of her new baby. When the baby is born, the mother enters another genesis; she is now a new mother who has the responsibility of protecting, nurturing and providing for her baby. Of course, the newborn has entered its first genesis as well, and this cycle will repeat itself over the course of their lives.

The genesis of every gift is the cave season; it is the season where we are undeveloped, immature, uncomfortable and unfamiliar with our surroundings. It is a season of concealment, darkness and frustration. An unborn infant, for example, is concealed in its mother's womb. The womb is dark, constricting and surrounded by water. As a matter of fact, twenty percent of human pregnancies end in miscarriage, and the majority of those miscarriages take place in the first trimester. All the same, most gifts repeatedly miscarry their assignments in the first trimester of a season. What is the assignment of the gift? It's the same assignment that the believer has and that is to destroy the works of the enemy, but of course, we do this by exercising our gifts and our faith.

One of the greatest strengths of the gift also doubles as the gift's most notable weakness. That strength is sensitivity. Creatives have heightened sensitivity, meaning, they tend to magnify what they see, sound, smell, taste and feel. For this reason, gifts are often easily offended and impatient, which consequentially, causes the gift to prematurely push out a plan, a business or a book. And while the gift may successfully launch a business, write a book or do something constructive, if the assignment was birthed in the wrong season, it can be considered stillborn. In other words, while it has the form and structure of a completed work, it has no life in it.

One of the reasons God hides gifts, especially during the onset of a new season, is because in any given era, there can be (and often is) a Pharaoh, Hitler, Hamen, Saul or Herod somewhere. These devil-possessed souls are drunk with power and overly determined to maintain their positions of power, meaning, they don't mind engaging in genocidal behavior if they believe a child, a person or a people will raise up and take their places. They aren't afraid of what you're currently doing, they are afraid of your potential! They are afraid of your future!

During the genesis of a creative's gifting, the creative is in the womb of his or her potential, and the creative's potential is in his or her womb. The gift (creative) is not hiding from the world; the gift is being hidden from the god of this world. 2 Corinthians 4:3-4 says it like this, "But if our gospel be hid, it is hid to them that are lost: In whom the god of this world hath blinded the minds of them which believe not, lest the light of the glorious gospel of Christ, who is the image of God, should shine unto them." Where is the gospel hidden? In you! You are the temple of the Holy Spirit; the Kingdom of God is within you! So, stop complaining about your seasons of obscurity. You aren't being ignored or punished! You aren't being rejected! You are being intentionally hidden! You can survive your genesis if you stop trying to reveal what God has been trying to conceal.

THE EXODUS OF A GIFT

The Greek word for *exodus* is *exodos* and it literally means departure. It means to exit or depart from a place. When the place is a wicked place and the person or people who are departing are believers, an exodus can be referenced as a deliverance. And, of course, the word *deliverance* simply means to save or to rescue.

We can exit a place in two ways—naturally or spiritually. As a matter of fact, deliverance must take place in two realms before it can be sustained. They are:
1. the natural realm
2. the realm of the spirit

In the natural realm, the heart has to shift in order for deliverance to begin. It doesn't have to immediately turn back to God, because deliverance is not always instantaneous; it is oftentimes both progressive and sequential. Progressive, meaning, it happens over time. Sequential, meaning, it happens in a specific order. Nevertheless, there must be some energy or force exerted in the heart that begins to move against what the heart once stood for. In the natural, we refer to this as friction.

According to Google, friction is, "the resistance that one surface or object encounters when moving over another." This is when the believer becomes conflicted within himself because his belief system is being moved upon by an even greater force. To get an illustration of what this looks like, consider the moment Jacob wrestled with an angel of the Lord. In Jacob's account, however, he went on record saying that he'd wrestled with God.

"And Jacob was left alone; and there wrestled a man with him until the breaking of the day. And when he saw that he prevailed not against him, he touched the hollow of his thigh; and the hollow of Jacob's thigh was out of joint, as he wrestled with him. And he said, Let me go, for the day breaketh. And he said, I will not let thee go, except thou bless me. And he said unto him, What is thy name? And he said, Jacob. And he said, Thy name shall be called no more Jacob, but Israel: for as a prince hast thou power with God and with men, and hast prevailed. And Jacob asked him, and said, Tell me, I pray thee, thy name. And he said, Wherefore is it that thou dost ask after my name? And he blessed him there. And Jacob called the name of the place Peniel: for I have seen God face to face, and my life is preserved."

Genesis 32:24-30

"The LORD hath also a controversy with Judah, and will punish Jacob according to his ways; according to his doings will he recompense him. He took his brother by the heel in the womb, and by his strength he had power with God: Yea, <u>he had power over the angel</u>, and prevailed: he wept, and made supplication unto him."

Hosea 12:2-4

The breaking of the day, as referenced in Genesis 32, denotes revelation. It means the revealing of a thing. Wrestling undoubtedly denotes two opposing forces. In the world of wrestling, the objective of the match can be simplified by one word: dominion. Dominion is a Kingdom term; it means to have governmental authority, sovereignty or control.

Man, within himself, is a government. He gets to authorize or legalize things in his life through agreement, just as he can veto anything that's been set in motion in his life by himself or his ancestors. He does this through repentance, deliverance and obedience. Man, within himself, is an enforcer of whatever laws he allows to govern his life. If any force works against his will, he has the legal authority to come against that force and arrest every authority that's creating friction in his life. Man, within himself, is a citizen of the world he's created for himself. Hosea said that Jacob had power over the angel. To understand this, you must first understand the backstory.

Jacob had once been a cunning man. He'd manipulated his brother out of his birthright and stolen the firstborn blessing that should have been reserved for Esau.

"And Jacob sod pottage: and Esau came from the field, and he was faint: And Esau said to Jacob, Feed me, I pray thee, with that same red pottage; for I am faint: therefore was his name called Edom. And Jacob said, Sell me this day thy birthright. And Esau said, Behold, I am at the point to die: and what profit shall this birthright do to me? And Jacob said, Swear to me this day; and he sware unto him: and he sold his birthright unto Jacob. Then Jacob gave Esau bread and pottage of lentiles; and he did eat and drink, and rose up, and went his way: thus Esau despised his birthright."
Genesis 25:29-34

"And it came to pass, as soon as Isaac had made an end of blessing Jacob, and Jacob was yet scarce gone out from the presence of Isaac his father, that Esau his brother came in from his hunting. And he also had made savoury meat, and brought it unto his father, and said unto his father, Let my father arise, and eat of his son's venison, that thy soul may bless me. And Isaac his father said unto him, Who art thou?

And he said, I am thy son, thy firstborn Esau. And Isaac trembled very exceedingly, and said, Who? where is he that hath taken venison, and brought it me, and I have eaten of all before thou camest, and have blessed him? yea, and he shall be blessed. And when Esau heard the words of his father, he cried with a great and exceeding bitter cry, and said unto his father, Bless me, even me also, O my father. And he said, Thy brother came with subtilty, and hath taken away thy blessing. And he said, Is not he rightly named Jacob? for he hath supplanted me these two times: he took away my birthright; and, behold, now he hath taken away my blessing. And he said, Hast thou not reserved a blessing for me? And Isaac answered and said unto Esau, Behold, I have made him thy lord, and all his brethren have I given to him for servants; and with corn and wine have I sustained him: and what shall I do now unto thee, my son? And Esau said unto his father, Hast thou but one blessing, my father? bless me, even me also, O my father. And Esau lifted up his voice, and wept."

Genesis 27:30-38

Because of Jacob's deceptive ways, his brother, Esau, vowed to kill him. This prompted Rebekkah to send Jacob into exile.

"And Esau hated Jacob because of the blessing wherewith his father blessed him: and Esau said in his heart, The days of mourning for my father are at hand; then will I slay my brother Jacob. And these words of Esau her elder son were told to Rebekah: and she sent and called Jacob her younger son, and said unto him, Behold, thy brother Esau, as touching thee, doth comfort himself, purposing to kill thee. Now therefore, my son, obey my voice; and arise, flee thou to Laban my brother to Haran; And tarry with him a few days, until thy brother's fury turn away; Until thy brother's anger turn away from thee, and he forget that which thou hast done to him: then I will send, and fetch thee from thence: why should I be deprived also of you both in one day?"

Genesis 27:41-45

Jacob eventually found himself in the company of someone who was more cunning than himself: Laban. Laban had two daughters: Leah and Rachel. The Bible refers to Leah as "weak-eyed", but it says that Rachel was both beautiful and well-favored. Having forgotten the seeds of deception he'd sown, Jacob had no reason to believe that his soon-to-be father-in-law would take advantage of him. For this reason, he asked Laban for his daughter Rachel, vowing to work for him for a total of seven years in exchange for her hand in marriage. In those days, it was customary for the man to pay what is referenced as a "bride price." Nevertheless, Jacob didn't have anything to give. He was on the run, and the only thing he could offer Laban was manual labor. Once the father of the soon-to-be bride agreed, he would enter into a contract with the groom-to-be. After this, the woman was betrothed or set aside for the groom-to-be. But Laban had other plans.

"And Jacob said unto Laban, Give me my wife, for my days are fulfilled, that I may go in unto her. And Laban gathered together all the men of the place, and made a feast. And it came to pass in the evening, that he took Leah his daughter, and brought her to him; and he went in unto her. And Laban gave unto his daughter Leah Zilpah his maid for an handmaid. And it came to pass, that in the morning, behold, it was Leah: and he said to Laban, What is this thou hast done unto me? Did not I serve with thee for Rachel? Wherefore then hast thou beguiled me? And Laban said, It must not be so done in our country, to give the younger before the firstborn. Fulfil her week, and we will give thee this also for the service which thou shalt serve with me yet seven other years. And Jacob did so, and fulfilled her week:

The Exodus of a Gift

and he gave him Rachel his daughter to wife also. And Laban gave to Rachel his daughter Bilhah his handmaid to be her maid. And he went in also unto Rachel, and he loved also Rachel more than Leah, and served with him yet seven other years."

Genesis 29:21-30

Now, as the story continues, we find Laban going out of his way to ensure that Jacob never stops working for him, but Jacob was determined to return to his father's house. After a dispute over cattle, the Lord spoke to Jacob and told him to return to the land of his fathers. This would be Jacob's exodus or way of escape. Jacob stole away his two wives, Rachel and Leah, his children and his cattle, and Rachel stole her father's gods. Three days later, Laban heard that his son-in-law had gone on the run, so he gathered up his sons and pursued him. Eventually, he found Jacob, and the two men argued, and then, eventually settled upon an agreement. After this, Jacob found himself journeying towards Edom to try to make peace with his brother, Esau. Jacob was terrified. He didn't know how Esau would respond to him. He'd been on the run for twenty years. Before Jacob would have his encounter with Esau, he would find himself wrestling with the angel of the Lord. And while that angel may have been set over that region (the Bible does not make this clear), it is evident that he was initially against Jacob's principles. Theologians have debated about the logic behind the wrestling match, but if you look at Jacob's life, Jacob had not been a devout man. Before this wrestling match, he was a con artist with a stolen inheritance. So, it can be argued that the wrestling was a picture of God taking down the old man (Jacob) and raising up the new man (Israel). Let's revisit the story.

"And Jacob was left alone; and there wrestled a man with him until the breaking of the day. And when he saw that he prevailed not against him, he touched the hollow of his thigh; and the hollow of Jacob's thigh was out of joint, as he wrestled with him. And he said, Let me go, for the day breaketh. And he said, I will not let thee go, except thou bless me. And he said unto him, What is thy name? And he said, Jacob. And he said, Thy name shall be called no more Jacob, but Israel: for as a prince hast thou power with God and with men, and hast prevailed. And Jacob asked him, and said, Tell me, I pray thee, thy name. And he said, Wherefore is it that thou dost ask after my name? And he blessed him there."

Genesis 32:24-29

God could not bless Jacob until he aligned himself with His will. That's when the old man Jacob, which means "supplanter" passed away and a new man was born. The word *supplant* literally means, "to take the place of (another), as through force, scheming, strategy, or the like. (2). To replace (one thing) by something else."
The name Israel means, "may God prevail."

Again, deliverance (or exodus) takes place in two realms:
1. in the natural
2. in the spirit

Jacob had wrestled with both natural and spiritual things over the course of his life. When he manipulated his brother out of his birthright, he took away his familial or natural governing authority. The birthright was often given to the firstborn, and it basically meant that he would take on the authority of his father. He would also receive a double portion of the inheritance left by his father. In other words, he'd get most of his father's material possessions. But the blessing of a father had everything to do with Kingdom authority. It was more than a natural blessing, it had everything to do with spiritual hierarchy or rank. It dealt with the patriarchal rule and rights transferred from a father to a son. Abraham blessed Isaac. Remember, God said to Abraham that he would be the father of many nations. Isaac then transferred this blessing, along with his patriarchal mantle.

"And he came near, and kissed him: and he smelled the smell of his raiment, and blessed him, and said, See, the smell of my son is as the smell of a field which the LORD hath blessed: <u>Therefore God give thee of the dew of Heaven</u>, and the fatness of the Earth, and plenty of corn and wine: <u>Let people serve thee, and nations bow down to thee: be lord over thy brethren, and let thy mother's sons bow down to thee</u>: cursed be every one that curseth thee, and blessed be he that blesseth thee."

Genesis 27:27-29

It needs to be understood that every region is subject to an authority. When a land, country or city is wicked, it is subject to a principality. A principality is a demonic governing authority that rules over a set of principles. Of course, every person who's subject to those principles (or beliefs) are subject to that principality. A belief or a group of beliefs that govern and are executed by a group of people in any given region is called a culture. Today, any time a believer has been given apostolic authority, that believer is charged to fight against principalities and ruling spirits. The word *apostle* means "sent one." Even though in the Old Testament, there were no apostles, many of the patriarchs of old had apostolic authority. So, when Jacob came near Edom and found himself wrestling with an angel of the Lord, he was wrestling with a belief system. Again, the angel wrestled with the old man (Jacob) and then blessed (empowered) the new man (Israel). Jacob, the man, had an inheritance from his father, Isaac, but Israel, the chosen one, had been granted the equivalent of apostolic authority.

The Exodus of a Gift

Every wrestler wants to dominate the match and overcome his opponent in the shortest amount of time possible. Wrestlers often have what's called their "advantage position." An advantage position is a position that allows one wrestler to execute dominion or gain control over the other. To gain an advantage over his opponent, one of the wrestlers must focus on his opponent's weakness. He does this by constantly shifting positions until he finds the one where his opponent can offer little to no resistance. The positioning of Jacob's heart was his weakness. He'd robbed his brother, married two daughters of a pagan man, and now, he wanted to reconcile with his brother. Nevertheless, his heart needed to be transformed. He needed to stop wrestling with God regarding who he was, and just return to the very place he'd once run away from. His wrestling match in the natural was symbolic of the mental wrestling match he'd been engaged in. He needed to surrender to God before he could take another step. All the same, because of the problems with his hip, Jacob could no longer run away from his problems. He would now have to face them head-on.

Let's consider a man going through deliverance. There must be a shifting of his perspective, but this shifting is not painless. It can be scary, exhausting and sometimes even humiliating. In order for this deliverance to be sustained, the individual receiving the deliverance has to increase his momentum in the things of God. In other words, if he didn't read his Bible before he received deliverance, it is vital that he starts reading the Word to sustain his deliverance. He has to begin actively pursuing the heart of God so that he can get in the will of God. He has to learn to stand against what he once stood for, and he has to learn to stand for what he once stood against. He has to confront what he once ran from. He must endure the friction, the confusion and the warfare that comes with a paradigmatic shift. As his heart continues to turn, his body starts behaving differently. What once made him laugh, now makes him cry. What once entertained him is now offensive to him. What he once called good, he now calls evil. What he once called up, he now calls down. This is the evidence of his deliverance.

Next, he must shift in the spirit. What does this entail or what does this mean? In the Kingdom of God, everything works through mutual consent. Another word for *mutual consent* is *agreement*. This principle is supported by scriptures detailing a few occasions when Jesus was about to perform a miracle. He would often ask the person who was in need of a miracle if he believed that He (the Lord) was able to perform it.

"And when Jesus departed thence, two blind men followed him, crying, and saying, Thou Son of David, have mercy on us. And when he was come into the house, the blind men came to him: and Jesus saith unto them, Believe ye that I am able to do this? They said unto him, Yea, Lord. Then touched he their eyes, saying, According to your faith be it unto you. And their eyes were opened."

Matthew 9:27-30

In other cases, the Lord would charge the individual to perform a certain act before receiving a miracle. This was an act of faith. For example, in Matthew 12:13, He told the man with a withered hand to stretch forth his hand. Doing this was a painful act; it required faith on the lame man's part. Before He resurrected a ruler's daughter, He said to the crowd of mourners who'd gathered to mourn her death, "Give place," which is another way of saying, "Get out." The Bible tells us that they'd laughed at Jesus when He told them that the young woman was not dead, but asleep. Therefore, when He told them to leave the room, He was pretty much instructing the ruler to relinquish his authority, after all, this was the ruler's house. Putting out the people who'd gathered to show him support would be an act of faith on his part. Remember this: Jesus will challenge you in the area in which you're the most or the least effective. The head of that home was a man of authority. Just like He'd told the lame man to stretch his hand forth, in Matthew 9, we find Jesus telling the ruler in so many words to stretch his authority. He had to surrender his authority to Jesus.

"And he said unto me, My grace is sufficient for thee: for my strength is made perfect in weakness."
2 Corinthians 12:9

Pharaoh refused to relinquish the authority he had over God's people. The Jews were entering the revelation or end of an old season, but they would first have to escape their Egyptian bondage. In today's deliverance terms, they needed to repent of their sins, after all, while a principality may rule over a region or a people, it is the spiritual wickedness in high places (idolatry) that gives the principality its legal authority.

"For we wrestle not against flesh and blood, but against principalities, against powers, against the rulers of the darkness of this world, against spiritual wickedness in high places."
Ephesians 6:12

Spiritual wickedness in high places denotes idolatry which, of course, took place in high places (mountaintops). The patriarchs of old had to tear down demonic altars and raise up altars for God. This was done for many reasons, but the main reason was to establish the will of God as the ruling authority over any given region or people. It was a place where a man of great authority linked his will (through faith) with God's will, thus, creating an agreement between Heaven and Earth. This was enough to dethrone a prince (principality) since principalities need an agreement (contract) between themselves and the people they are attempting to rule over.

An exodus is the gap between two worlds or realities. It is the dethroning of one god and the crowning of another. When Moses stood in front of the Red Sea, he was at the height of yet another exodus. He was about to lead the people of God out of their place of bondage into a new season (genesis). But there was a problem with this deliverance. The problem was, the people had not embraced the revelation of the old season. Like many believers today, they were eager to escape the bondage that they'd been under, but they'd adopted the ways, culture and reasoning of their enemy. For this reason, they were not entirely against the Egyptians and what they stood for. In other words, an agreement was still in place, and even though their enemies were now dead, the Jews found themselves still soul-tied to them. They were still in love with an old season. They walked towards the promised land, all the while, reminiscing about their past. Think of it this way—as they crossed over that narrow space that God created when He split the Red Sea for them, they were walking down the aisle towards God, all the while, reminiscing about their former lover: Egypt. They were double-minded lovers who wanted both the benefits of the Kingdom and the pleasures of their old lives.

Another way to look at an exodus is to think about a breakup or divorce. According to social scientists, the five stages of grief that follow a divorce are:
- denial
- anger
- bargaining
- depression
- acceptance

The Exodus of a Gift

These are the many regions (or dimensions) that a recent divorcee must venture through.

Denial: in this season, the soul is caught between two worlds or two kingdoms. The individual has trouble accepting his or her new reality, and for this reason, the person may move forward naturally, but refuse to move on mentally or dimensionally. This is because, during this stage, the lines (boundaries) between both worlds are blurred. Denial serves both as a temporary coping mechanism and a sound check of the soul. It is during this phase that most people decide whether they want to return to whatever or whoever it is that they've estranged themselves from.

Some great examples of denial take place in the story detailing the destruction of Sodom and Gomorrah (see Genesis 19). In this story, we find a few souls who have trouble letting go of the very thing that God is trying to deliver them from, and these people are Lot and his wife.

"And the men said unto Lot, Hast thou here any besides? son in law, and thy sons, and thy daughters, and whatsoever thou hast in the city, bring them out of this place: For we will destroy this place, because the cry of them is waxen great before the face of the LORD; and the LORD hath sent us to destroy it. And Lot went out, and spake unto his sons in law, which married his daughters, and said, Up, get you out of this place; for the LORD will destroy this city. But he seemed as one that mocked unto his sons in law."
Genesis 19:12-14

The above passage denotes a divorce between one reality and another. In this, we find the angels of the Lord warning Lot and telling him to take his family and leave Sodom.

"And when the morning arose, then the angels hastened Lot,

saying, Arise, take thy wife, and thy two daughters, which are here; lest thou be consumed in the iniquity of the city. And while he lingered, the men laid hold upon his hand, and upon the hand of his wife, and upon the hand of his two daughters; the LORD being merciful unto him: and they brought him forth, and set him without the city."

Genesis 19:15-16

We can see denial manifesting itself in Lot's procrastination. The scriptures say the angels "hastened Lot," meaning, he was moving too slow and "while he lingered, the men laid hold upon his hand." When the human mind is forced to cross from one dimension to another, it often copes by lingering. We call this dwelling on the past or refusing to move on. When it's mixed with anger, we call this unforgiveness. All the same, Lot's wife had trouble moving on as well, but her denial didn't manifest itself as procrastination, it manifested itself as rebellion.

"But his wife looked back from behind him, and she became a pillar of salt."

Genesis 19:26

One of the manifestations of denial is looking back. This is a season within a season where the soul can't move on because the person keeps looking back at what God is trying to deliver him or her from. It is during this phase that we find ourselves on our exes' social media pages, clicking on everyone we believe they may be romantically linked to. It is during this phase that we find ourselves calling our exes' loved ones or friends, hoping to tell our sides of the story. It is also during this phase that we incessantly take our exes to court, demanding everything from child support to child custody, in hopes of extending the last season.

Anger: in this season, the soul begins to sober up to its new reality. The sight of the old season is still very much in sight, and the scent of the old season is still fresh. During this phase, most people find themselves getting angry with God and anyone they believe to be responsible for them being exiled from their previous seasons. It is during this phase that the soul has started accepting that he or she is truly being rejected. Let's use a man, for example. Estranged from his former lover, he finds himself thinking about every accusation and every negative word that's been uttered. He finds himself thinking about all the good he's done, and all the bad his estranged lover has done. Even when he thinks about the evils he's done in the relationship, it's hard for him to come to terms with the end results. In his mind, the crime does not match the punishment. In his mind, the greater evil is the breakup itself. Everything else could have been worked out. Even if he's the one who ended the relationship, he still feels robbed of his time, his trust and everything that he holds dear to him. It is hard for him, in that moment, to fully accept that the relationship is truly over.

There are four stages a wound must go through to heal. They are:
1. **Hemostasis:** this is the first stage of healing. Hemostasis occurs when the blood begins to clot behind the fresh wound to stop it from bleeding. Another name for this is coagulation.
2. **Inflammatory:** the body begins to work toward destroying bacteria and removing any foreign debris. In other words, the body releases its warrior cells—the white blood cells to fight off anything that may cause an infection. This is to prepare the wounded area for the growth of new tissue.
3. **Proliferative:** this stage has three phases: the first is to fill the wound, the next one is to contract the wound's margins and the final phase is to cover the wound.
4. **Maturation:** during this stage, the new tissue begins

to strengthen and gain more flexibility.

Of course, the healing process can be interrupted if the wound is inflamed or the person is injured again in or around that same area. It can also be interrupted if the person scratches it when it begins to itch. Itching occurs as a wound begins to heal. It is the result of the wound being pulled shut by cells that have bonded together.

Anger is the inflammatory stage of healing. This is when the individual is the most sensitive, and feels the need to defend himself the most.

Bargaining: during this stage of an exodus, the individual is caught between two worlds. He knows that he should move on and heal, but he's made a lot of investments in the world he's coming out of. This is the stage of consideration. This is the stage where he may find himself pleading with God, pleading with his estranged lover or trying to find some way to silence his heart. He will consider changing his ways or accepting the demands of his estranged lover. During this stage, he is riddled with guilt and shame. Despite how he feels, nevertheless, he can also see the light of his new season, but the problem is, the land ahead, while beautiful, looks unfamiliar and lonely.

Depression: this is the stage where he may find himself hosting many feelings at one time. This is the phase when all of his emotions converge to create a very noisy storm. One day, he's sad, another day, he's lonely, the next day, he's glad, and by the end of the week, he's angry. These emotions create a fog that seems to loom over him for weeks or months on end. His soul is beginning to settle and accept its new reality, and while the sounds and smells of the old season are still faintly there, he still has trouble understanding why things happened the way that they did.

The depression stage is the one that seems to be the stickiest. Many men and women get stuck in this stage because they can have days or weeks of happiness, followed by a few days of sadness. Thinking this is normal, many people settle in this phase, never truly accepting their new realities. In short, this is the equivalent of their forty years in the wilderness—a wilderness that should have taken them eleven days to come out of.

Acceptance: This is the stage right before revelation. While the individual may not have all the answers, he has finally accepted his new reality. He's finally made peace with the fact that his former plans were not God's plans for him. This is the stage where he walks into his promised land. This is the maturation stage of the healing process. He's gotten a wealth of wisdom, knowledge and understanding from his former season, and now, he's ready to move forward into his season of revelation.

THE REVELATION OF A GIFT

"An uncovering, a bringing to light of that which had been previously wholly hidden or only obscurely seen. God has been pleased in various ways and at different times (Hebrews 1:1) to make a supernatural revelation of himself and his purposes and plans, which, under the guidance of his Spirit, has been committed to writing. The Scriptures are not merely the 'record' of revelation; they are the revelation itself in a written form, in order to the accurate preservation and propagation of the truth.

Revelation and inspiration differ. Revelation is the supernatural communication of truth to the mind; inspiration (q.v.) secures to the teacher or writer infallibility in communicating that truth to others. It renders its subject the spokesman or prophet of God in such a sense that everything he asserts to be true, whether fact or doctrine or moral principle, is true, infallibly true."
(Source: Bible Study Tools/ Dictionaries/ Quick Reference Dictionary/ Revelation)

The time between the genesis of a gift to the revelation of that gift is called a journey. On a journey, there are many paths to take, but it is up to the sojourner to choose which path he or she believes to be the right one. Notice that the patriarchs of the Bible never settled in one place; they went from one geographical location to another. In the Old Testament, they journeyed from one land to another, building altars for God and having tangible encounters with

Him. In the New Testament, the Apostles traveled around the world spreading the gospel of Jesus Christ. Every man's journey was centered around deliverance, and every man's journey was orchestrated to develop him as a leader. This way, he could lead the people of God, either by foot or by principle.

In this chapter, my goal is to help you to see the history and process of revelation or, better yet, how God reveals a thing. In this chapter, I'm going to share a few biblical stories with you so that you can get a better grasp of your own personal chapter of revelation.

Everything that is revealed was once hidden. Every revelation was once a secret or a mystery. For example, a parable is a truth hidden in a story—a story that was told by Jesus to teach a moral or spiritual lesson. When Jesus's disciples asked Him why He spoke to the people in parables, He answered with, "Because it is given to you to know the mysteries of the kingdom of Heaven, but to them it is not given. For whoever has, to him shall be given, and he shall have more abundance: but whoever has not, from him shall be taken away even that he has. Therefore speak I to them in parables: because they seeing see not; and hearing they hear not, neither do they understand" (Matthew 13:11-13).

The book of Revelations, like Genesis, is one of the most interesting books in the Bible because it details many of the supernatural events that will precede what we so commonly refer to as Armageddon. This is the one book that you won't find too many leaders preaching about on Sunday morning because it is shrouded in mystery. Let's look at one of the parables told in the book of Revelations.

"And a great sign was seen in Heaven: a woman arrayed with the sun, and the moon under her feet, and upon her

The Revelation of a Gift

head a crown of twelve stars; and she was with child; and she crieth out, travailing in birth, and in pain to be delivered. And there was seen another sign in Heaven: and behold, a great red dragon, having seven heads and ten horns, and upon his heads seven diadems. And his tail draweth the third part of the stars of Heaven, and did cast them to the Earth: and the dragon standeth before the woman that is about to be delivered, that when she is delivered he may devour her child.
And she was delivered of a son, a man child, who is to rule all the nations with a rod of iron: and her child was caught up unto God, and unto his throne. And the woman fled into the wilderness, where she hath a place prepared of God, that there they may nourish her a thousand two hundred and threescore days.
And there was war in Heaven: Michael and his angels going forth to war with the dragon; and the dragon warred and his angels; And they prevailed not, neither was their place found any more in Heaven. And the great dragon was cast down, the old serpent, he that is called the Devil and Satan, the deceiver of the whole world; he was cast down to the Earth, and his angels were cast down with him. And I heard a great voice in Heaven, saying, Now is come the salvation, and the power, and the kingdom of our God, and the authority of his Christ: for the accuser of our brethren is cast down, who accuseth them before our God day and night. And they overcame him because of the blood of the Lamb, and because of the word of their testimony; and they loved not their life even unto death. Therefore rejoice, O Heavens, and ye that dwell in them. Woe for the Earth and for the sea: because the devil is gone down unto you, having great wrath, knowing that he hath but a short time.

Revelation 12:1-12

Many historians and theologians have tried to unpack or unveil the mystery behind this story. Nevertheless, this parable details much more than what meets the eye. So, let's see what we can extract from it.

Who is the woman clothed with the sun? Mary, the mother of Jesus, of course.
Why is she wearing a crown of twelve stars? The twelve stars represent the twelve tribes of Israel.
Why did the dragon have seven heads and ten horns? The seven heads represent the seven mountains of influence. The ten horns represent ten kings or ten rulers who will arise.
Why did it have seven diadems? What do they represent? Diadems are crowns traditionally worn by women, however, in the biblical text, it simply means crown. So, the dragon ruled over the seven mountains of influence. As a church, our assignment is to gain control over each mountain. He is our Goliath. What did David do to Goliath after defeating him? He cut off his head!
Who was this man-child that she was pregnant with—the man who would rule all the nations with a rod of iron? Jesus Christ!
How was the child caught up to God? After Jesus's crucifixion, He was in the earth for three days. After that, He walked the earth for forty days before being caught up to God.

What is the mystery behind Revelation 12? This chapter details the fall of Satan; this fall occurred when Jesus's blood was shed. Revelation 12:10-11 reads, "And I heard a great voice in Heaven, saying, Now is come the salvation, and the power, and the kingdom of our God, and the authority of his Christ: for the accuser of our brethren is cast down, who accuseth them before our God day and night. And they overcame him because of the blood of the Lamb, and because of the word of their testimony; and they loved not their life even unto death." In short, this event already took place! This parable is rich with so much more revelation, but this revelation can only be received by the sons and daughters of God.

You are a gift. Traditionally, in the Western world, when we give a gift to someone, we box it up, wrap it with decorative paper, seal that paper so that the gift is not easily opened, and then, we give it to the receiver on the appointed day. We don't want them to know what's in the box because we want it to be a surprise. Most adults can attest to the fact that opening a gift before the appointed day, while exciting, can prove to be disappointing. For example, most of us have had the opportunity to open a Christmas gift before Christmas or a birthday gift before our birthdays. Because of impatience, we begged our parents, guardians or whoever it was that gave us the gift for the opportunity to at least peek at the gift. When they agreed, we happily ripped the paper off the gift and ripped through the box. After that, we shouted for joy after revealing what was once hidden behind the beautiful gift wrap. A few days or weeks later, Christmas came or our birthdays arrived, and we were left feeling like we hadn't gotten anything. Because of this, we felt unappreciated, discouraged and sometimes even upset. This is because we opened our gifts prematurely.

Just like Revelation 12, you are jam-packed with mysteries just waiting to be revealed. You can sense the wealth in you; you can somehow sense that there's so much more to you than what meets the eye. This is the reason you became restless in your previous relationships. The relationship had piqued, and the man or woman you were with at that time could not see your value. Truth be told, you couldn't see your value, but you could sense it. You went to church, and while the pastor was preaching, you learned a little bit more about yourself. You read a few articles and learned that you're an introvert, extrovert or ambivert. You studied the characteristics of whichever class you fell under, and this

The Revelation of a Gift

helped you to understand so much more about your personality. You went from one relationship to another, one organization to another, one job to another and one friendship to another trying to discover the totality of who you are. You kept finding pieces of yourself, but it was never enough to answer the many questions that you have. Every relationship, job and concept that you entered was a box, meaning, it was a limited space. Why would you try to box yourself in? The answer is found in 1 Corinthians 2:9, which reads, "But as it is written, eye hath not seen, nor ear heard, neither have entered into the heart of man, the things which God hath prepared for them that love him." In other words, your mind doesn't have the capacity to understand God's plans for you, so in your attempt to unbox your identity, you settled for what you could conceptualize. You prayed, you fasted and you impatiently waited for God to reveal the mystery that is you. Nevertheless, His answers didn't come fast enough, so you found yourself in yet another relationship looking for affirmation or confirmation. But your new lover still couldn't figure you out. Your new friend couldn't figure you out. Why is this? It's because you are a gift, but unlike a natural present, God only appoints specific people to unravel your potential, and the full unboxing of who you are can take a lifetime to complete itself. Howbeit, you have to go through the valleys of each season until you reach the revelation of those seasons.

People have tried unsuccessfully to figure you out. There was even a season when you thought that someone would lay their hands on you (in prayer) and God would reveal your potential to them. This didn't happen. When you got up off the floor, you went back to your seat still struggling to understand the fullness of who you are and why you do the things that you do. Why are you more passionate about somethings than others? Why is it that people come up with a bunch of theories regarding your character, only to discover later that they were completely off? Again, the answer is, your life is shrouded in mystery. Another facet of your identity is revealed at the conclusion of each season that you enter, and it is only revealed to specific people.

Every parable, just like every Kingdom mystery, has a lesson behind it, but to get to the meat of that lesson, we need the season of revelation. Howbeit, to navigate that season, we need the fruit of the Holy Spirit. Galatians 5:22 tells us what those fruit are. It reads, "But the fruit of the Spirit is love, joy, peace, longsuffering (which means patience), kindness, goodness, faithfulness, meekness, self-control; against such there is no law."

Let's focus on one of these fruits: patience. If we are honest with ourselves, patience, while it is a virtue and a fruit of the Holy Spirit, is a word that looks better written out than it does walked out. This is because the space, period or journey between glory to glory and victory to victory requires us to give up more of ourselves, our desires and our plans. Let's look at it this way. I want you to imagine glory being the buzzer at the top of a high mountain. To get to it, you've had to go through the valleys or low places, and then, you've had to ascend the mountain. This ascension wasn't easy, nor was it glamorous; it was soul-wrenching, time-consuming and frustrating. Nevertheless, you made it to the top, pushed the buzzer, and now, your next assignment is to push the buzzer on the mountain that's next to the mountain you're on. The space between the two mountains is wide, so you can't jump from glory to glory. Instead, you have to descend the mountain you're on, which lands you back in the valley of decision. From there, you have to take another painstaking journey, and then, ascend yet another mountain. The space or time between both mountains is called a season. Why does God cause us to go through these valleys? It's to get us to develop the fruit of the Spirit, of course. This is so that when He fully unpacks our potential, the people in our lives will see and glorify Him. So, the journey or space between two seasons is all about killing the fruit of the flesh.

"Now the works of the flesh are manifest, which are these : fornication, uncleanness, lasciviousness, idolatry, sorcery, enmities, strife, jealousies, wraths, factions, divisions, parties, envyings, drunkenness, revellings, and such like; of which I forewarn you, even as I did forewarn you, that they who practise such things shall not inherit the kingdom of God."

Galatians 5:19-21

Let's consider the Garden of Eden. It was a garden filled with good fruit, but there was one tree that God told Adam and Eve to avoid. He told them to not eat from the Tree of the Knowledge of Good and Evil. The fruit on that tree wasn't necessarily bad. The evil, at that time, was in the act, not in the fruit found on the tree. Once you know something, you are held accountable for it. Peter said it this way, "For it were better for them not to have known the way of righteousness, than, after knowing it, to turn back from the holy commandment delivered unto them" (2 Peter 2:21). God didn't want Adam and Eve to have the knowledge of good and evil. He wanted them to remain innocent; He wanted them to remain spotless. Nevertheless, the couple decided that they wanted to embrace the forbidden knowledge instead.

We all know the story. Satan deceived Eve and she ate from the Tree of the Knowledge of Good and Evil, and then, she took the fruit to her husband, Adam. He then ate some of the fruit as well, and because of this, God evicted the rebellious couple from the Garden. The journey then became about them trying to find their way back to the Garden. But Eden is not a physical locale; it is a realm within the Kingdom.

The Revelation of a Gift

Eden is God's garden. Adam and Eve were the couple charged with keeping the Garden. Genesis 2:4-7 reads, "These are the generations of the Heavens and of the Earth when they were created, in the day that the LORD God made the Earth and the Heavens, and every plant of the field before it was in the Earth, and every herb of the field before it grew: for the LORD God had not caused it to rain upon the earth, <u>and there was not a man to till the ground</u>. But there went up a mist from the earth, and watered the whole face of the ground. And the LORD God formed man of the dust of the ground, and breathed into his nostrils the breath of life; and man became a living soul."

Adam's job was to till the ground of the Garden. But to do this, he had to be in agreement with God, after all, he would essentially reproduce himself in that Garden. What do we do when we find a bad plant in our gardens? We chop it down, uproot it and cast it out! When the couple disobeyed God, they didn't just start bearing bad fruit, they became bad fruit. So, God kicked them out of Eden and their new assignment began. They were now in charge of their own personal gardens. They now had the knowledge of good and evil. Their assignment then became about them overseeing and overcoming themselves and teaching their children to do the same. The war was no longer on the outskirts of their conscious; it suddenly came from within. They now had to wrestle with the works or, better yet, fruit of the flesh. Galatians 5:19-21 tells us (once again) what those fruit are. "Now the works of the flesh are manifest, which are these : fornication, uncleanness, lasciviousness, idolatry, sorcery, enmities, strife, jealousies, wraths, factions, divisions, parties, envyings, drunkenness, revellings, and such like; of which I forewarn you, even as I did forewarn you, that they who practise such things shall not inherit the kingdom of God."

The Revelation of a Gift

Adam and Eve would have children who would venture further and further away from God (in concept), but the goal was to get them to come back into agreement with their First Love. This process is called repentance. Knowledge precedes repentance. I cannot repent for a sin unless I first *know* it is a sin, and secondly, I must know the correct response. This gives me the ability to make a sound choice. If I choose to sin against God, I then plant the seed of rebellion in my life. If I choose to obey God, I plant the fruits of the Spirit in my life. Essentially, what I'm doing is creating a garden, only, the garden is within me.

We were created from dirt, therefore, whenever we believe something, we plant it in our hearts and reproduce it. When we reject something, we uproot it or prevent it from taking root in our lives. Our obvious assignment is to create a Garden of Eden (of sorts) within ourselves, and this garden must be filled with the fruit of the Spirit. This is something the people who tried to build the Tower of Babel did not understand. They were chasing religion instead of revelation. They thought that if they built a structure that reached up to Heaven that they would be able to shove their way back into God's presence, but not His will (many believers today still attempt to bully God by threatening to not serve Him should they not get their way). What they didn't realize is that Heaven isn't up; it's around us and within us. For this reason, they spent 107 years building the Tower of Babel, only to have God come along and confuse their language. Understand this—if what you're building with the people in your life does not bring you to repentance, God will intervene. His goal is to get you to the end of a season where He can reveal Himself and the purpose of that season to you. Sure, you may tell your new beau or your new girl everything you know about yourself, but this is not enough revelation to sustain a lifelong relationship. God only reveals you to the right people in the right season.

"And they said, Go to, let us build us a city and a tower, whose top may reach to Heaven; and let us make us a name, lest we be scattered abroad on the face of the whole Earth. And the LORD came down to see the city and the tower, which the children of men built. And the LORD said, <u>Behold, the people is one</u>, and they <u>have all one language</u>; and this they begin to do: and now nothing will be restrained from them, which they have imagined to do. Go to, let us go down, and there <u>confound their language</u>, that they may not understand one another's speech. So <u>the LORD scattered them abroad</u> from there on the face of all the Earth: and they left off to build the city. Therefore is the name of it called Babel; because the LORD did there confound the language of all the Earth: and from there did the LORD <u>scatter them abroad on the face of all the Earth</u>."
Genesis 11:4-9

One of the grave mistakes that the people made was that they tried to get to Heaven without having the heart of God. They tried to build a tower, instead of ascending a mountain, creating an altar and giving God what was due to Him. In other words, they tried to break into Heaven. "Verily, verily, I say unto you, He that entereth not by the door into the fold of the sheep, but climbeth up some other way, the same is a thief and a robber" (John 10:1).

Again, God is all about unity, but if you're building a concept, relationship, business or any type of structure with anyone outside of God's will, He will disrupt your plans by altering the communication between you and the person or people that you're building with. While He is a God of unity, He is also a God who divides. He divides the righteous from the unrighteous, the darkness from the light, the seen from the unseen and the natural from the supernatural. Religion has taught us that He is the God of unity, but rarely are we introduced to the divisive side of God. The word *divisive* has some negative connotations to it, but if you understand that God is good, you will also understand that if He's dividing anything, it's for a good reason. Below are a few scriptures to help us see the divisive or, better yet, strategic side of God.

"And God said, Let there be lights in the firmament of the Heaven to divide the day from the night."
Genesis 1:14

"Think not that I am come to send peace on Earth: I came not to send peace, but a sword. For I am come to set a man at variance *against* his father, and the daughter *against* her mother, and the daughter in law against her mother in law. And a man's foes shall be they of his own household."
Matthew 10:34-36

God will devise and execute a plan to get you from glory to glory or, better yet, revelation to revelation. He is strategic, creative and intentional, and as such, He is always dividing, adding, multiplying and subtracting. He does this so that He can bring us to a place of awareness. We become more aware of His presence, more aware of our purpose and more aware of how the Kingdom of God operates. It is here that He can reveal more of His heart to us. It is here that He can reveal the mysteries of Heaven with us. It is here that He can reveal the secrets to our identities to us. God strategically places gifts in caves so that He can reveal Himself to and through them at the appointed time. Let's consider the story of Noah. The flood took place seven hundred years before mankind attempted to build the Tower of Babel.

"And God said to Noah, The end of all flesh is come before me; for the Earth is filled with violence through them; and, behold, I will destroy them with the Earth. Make you an ark of gopher wood; rooms shall you make in the ark, and shall pitch it within and without with pitch. And this is the fashion which you shall make it of: The length of the ark shall be three hundred cubits, the breadth of it fifty cubits, and the height of it thirty cubits. A window shall you make to the ark, and in a cubit shall you finish it above; and the door of the ark shall you set in the side thereof; with lower, second, and third stories shall you make it. And, behold, I, even I, do bring a flood of waters on the Earth, to destroy all flesh, wherein is the breath of life, from under Heaven; and every thing that is in the Earth shall die. But with you will I establish my covenant; and you shall come into the ark, you, and your sons, and your wife, and your sons' wives with you. And of every living thing of all flesh, two of every sort shall you bring into the ark, to keep them alive with you; they shall be male and female. Of fowls after their kind, and of cattle after their kind, of every creeping thing of the Earth after his kind, two of every sort shall come to you, to keep them alive. And take you to you of all food that is eaten, and you shall gather it to you; and it shall be for food for you, and for them. Thus did Noah; according to all that God commanded him, so did he."

Genesis 6:13-22

"And Noah was six hundred years old when the flood of waters was on the Earth. And Noah went in, and his sons, and his wife, and his sons' wives with him, into the ark, because of the waters of the flood. Of clean beasts, and of beasts that are not clean, and of fowls, and of every thing that creeps on the Earth, There went in two and two to Noah into the ark, the male and the female, as God had commanded Noah. And it came to pass after seven days, that the waters of the flood were on the Earth. In the six hundredth year of Noah's life, in the second month, the seventeenth day of the month, the same day were all the fountains of the great deep broken up, and the windows of Heaven were opened. And the rain was on the Earth forty days and forty nights."

Genesis 7:6-12

In short, the Bible tells us that Noah walked with God, meaning, he was in agreement with God. (Can two walk together except they be agreed?) Noah was a just man. This also means that he was probably an odd guy, seeing as it is that he had not conformed to the ever-so-present evils around him. Instead, Noah chose to serve God with all of his heart and with all his household.

When did Noah's cave season start? Most people would theorize that Noah's ark was his cave, but this is partially true. Noah was a righteous gift living amongst unrighteous people who were blind to his potential. More than likely, Noah wasn't a popular man. He undoubtedly appeared to be a religious lunatic to the people around him. This essentially means that Noah's life before the flood had been a time of concealment for him. When the Bible says that Noah walked with God, it's pretty much saying that he spent time with God. This was Noah's cave season. When Noah started building the ark, however, his cave season started coming to an end. In that moment, he had to do the one thing that many of us take for granted—he had to make a sacrifice. He sacrificed what was left of his identity, he sacrificed what was left of his reputation and he likely sacrificed the respect of those closest to him. Can you imagine the stares, the rumors, the criticism and the humiliation that Noah and his household had to endure? And if this wasn't bad enough, he then had to be seen marching through town with a bunch of wild animals taking them towards the ark he'd built. Can you imagine what Noah and his sons must've looked like trying to drag alligators towards an unusually large ship? Noah, to the people around him, looked like he'd lost his mind. Nevertheless, he didn't let this sway him. He kept obeying God.

Eventually, Noah entered the ark and shut the door. He shut the door on his last season and prepared to go into the next one. He was about to begin his journey out of his cave. What was he doing? He was, in essence, saying what Christ would say thousands of years later— "It is finished!" This means that he'd completed his assignment. He'd built the ship, brought two animals of every kind into the ark and loaded his family into it. As the rain began to fall, the people who'd once laughed at and scorned him came to the sobering realization that he wasn't a madman after all. In their moment of revelation, they realized that Noah was a true prophet of the Most High God, but by that time, it was too late. He'd shut the door behind him, much like the bridegroom had done in Matthew 25:10, leaving the five foolish maidens locked out. Here's a principle. Anytime a season ends in your life, God will have you to shut some doors. There are some people who will never know what God placed on the inside of you. Then again, there are some people who will one day see your potential, but they will no longer be able to benefit from it.

After the waters subsided, Noah found himself in the genesis of his next chapter. Genesis 8:13-22 reads, "And it came to pass in the six hundredth and first year, in the first month, the first day of the month, the waters were dried up from off the Earth: and Noah removed the covering of the ark, and looked, and, behold, the face of the ground was dry. And in the second month, on the seven and twentieth day of the month, was the Earth dried. And God spoke to Noah, saying, Go forth of the ark, you, and your wife, and your sons, and your sons' wives with you. Bring forth with you every living thing that is with you, of all flesh, both of fowl, and of cattle, and of every creeping thing that creeps on the

The Revelation of a Gift

Earth; that they may breed abundantly in the Earth, and be fruitful, and multiply on the Earth. And Noah went forth, and his sons, and his wife, and his sons' wives with him: Every beast, every creeping thing, and every fowl, and whatever creeps on the Earth, after their kinds, went forth out of the ark. And Noah built an altar to the LORD; and took of every clean beast, and of every clean fowl, and offered burnt offerings on the altar. And the LORD smelled a sweet smell; and the LORD said in his heart, I will not again curse the ground any more for man's sake; for the imagination of man's heart is evil from his youth; neither will I again smite any more every thing living, as I have done. While the Earth remains, seedtime and harvest, and cold and heat, and summer and winter, and day and night shall not cease."

Noah's unboxing, of course, hadn't ended. It had just begun. When he opened the windows of the ark, revelation hit him where he stood. Revelations 21:1 reads, "And I saw a new Heaven and a new Earth: for the first Heaven and the first Earth are passed away; and the sea is no more." Of course, this is the account from the Apostle John's vision, but you can see that in Noah's moment of revelation, this was his testimony as well. The waters had subsided. He was now in a new chapter, and we'd all love to believe that his life was perfect after this. Nevertheless, he'd have to endure new problems. Sure, we go from glory to glory, but the journey or space between the two is called a valley. A valley is a low place between two hills or mountains. For believers, on the other hand, a valley is synonymous with a low place mentally and/or spiritually. A valley is what connects one season with another. Noah would find himself in a few more valleys over the course of his life, with one of those valleys being the moment his son, Ham, decided to expose him, instead of covering him.

"And Noah began to be a husbandman, and planted a vineyard: and he drank of the wine, and was drunken. And he was uncovered within his tent. And Ham, the father of Canaan, saw the nakedness of his father, and told his two brethren without. And Shem and Japheth took a garment, and laid it upon both their shoulders, and went backward, and covered the nakedness of their father. And their faces were backward, and they saw not their father's nakedness. And Noah awoke from his wine, and knew what his youngest son had done unto him.
And he said, Cursed be Canaan; A servant of servants shall he be unto his brethren."

Genesis 9:20-25

After Noah confronted his son Ham, we didn't hear anything else about him, even though he lived well over four hundred years after that incident. The cave had prepared him for that one heightened moment—the moment when he'd have to endure the ridicule of men and build an ark. The cave had prepared him for the heartbreak he undoubtedly felt as the waters rose, lifting the ship up from the Earth. Noah lost people that he loved in that flood as well. He was able to save his wife, his sons and his sons' wives, but the Bible didn't mention anything about any daughters he may have had. Of course, we don't know if he had any daughters at that time. It is possible that he did, but he'd married them off. I'm sure that he also had to listen to the agonizing cries of his daughters-in-law. They'd lost their loved ones. The point is, we don't hear anything else about Noah after he cursed Canaan, his grandson. This means that God can place you in a cave, allow you to endure humiliation, loneliness, criticism and persecution, all in preparation for one big revelatory event in your life. After that event has come and gone, it is a possibility that you may go on to lead a "normal" life. This doesn't mean the fullness of your potential has been unpacked; it simply means that every other event pales in comparison to the one where God used you mightily.

One of the commonalities you'll notice in many of these stories is the presence of water. God has repeatedly used water throughout the scriptures to symbolize:
1. the washing of the Word, cleansing
2. salvation or eternal life
3. the Spirit of God
4. the fountains of living water
5. new birth

Before a mother gives birth to an infant, she is in one of the most painful, dreadful and agonizing moments of her life, and in that moment, her unborn child is in his or her exodus. Before the infant passes through her womb, the mother's water is supposed to break. (Note: there have been some cases of women giving birth without the amniotic sac breaking, but this is rare.) This water helps to lubricate the birth canal so that the baby can pass through it. During the labor, the mother is at the end of a season, and she's about to enter a new season. Her gift is just minutes, hours or days away from being revealed, but before this happens, she must push. She has to put pressure on her womb when she feels a contraction. In other words, despite the pain she's in, she still has a role in her child's deliverance. She can't just lay still and complain, after all, faith without works is dead. Additionally, she has to listen to the voice of her coach: the midwife or doctor. In that moment, her coach's voice is often annoying, but it is absolutely important that she listens to the coach to ensure, not only her safety, but a safe delivery of her child. The birthing of a child is very similar to the birthing of a new season. It can be distressing, painful and overwhelming, but on the other side of that pain is a blessing.

Before every exodus or transition is a season of normality, and this season is often followed by a season of frustration and distress. During our seasons of normality, we have either accepted our realities or we've come to love our lives as they are. We've become content with the people and things we have access to. Additionally, we have learned to navigate the seasons that we're in so well that we often become prideful or we may find ourselves flirting with pride. This is the reason Apostle Paul said in 1 Corinthians 8:1 that knowledge puffs people up. Think about it this way—when a man lives in a small city his entire life, he becomes a danger to himself and others because he's learned to navigate the roads of that city by memory. For this reason, he'll often be found speeding down the roads without paying too much attention to the traffic signs, pedestrians or anything that dares to venture out onto his path. If he's familiar with the patterns of his city's law enforcement, he will likely run stop signs, red lights and speed past yield signs every time he gets behind the wheel of his car. This is what familiarity does to a man. It causes him to become puffed up and careless.

Behind the season of normality is oftentimes a season of frustration. Of course, frustration is often brought on by change or the threat of change. A content man becomes contentious when his routine has been altered. He can no longer rely on his knowledge once change has occurred; instead, he has to start relying on others. For example, the man living in a small city may be able to navigate the roads of his city without fail if those roads haven't been changed in years. Nevertheless, if the city decides to close some old roads and open some new ones, the man in question has no choice but to slow down and pay attention. God knows this, and it is for this reason that He will remove or add someone or something in our lives just to instigate our exoduses from one mindset to another.

The Revelation of a Gift

YAHWEH called Jonah out of his season of normality. The Lord told Jonah to go to Ninevah and cry against it because the place had become wicked. Jonah was a gift, but he didn't want to answer the call on his life. He wanted to continue in his previous season, so he went to Joppa, paid the fare to get on a ship that was headed to Tarshish and he boarded the ship. While on the ship, a storm began to rage, and that storm was too much for the ship to withstand. This ship was nothing like the ark Noah had built, and the storm was far more unforgiving than the one Noah had overcome. Of course, this is because Noah had obeyed God, whereas, Jonah was in the midst of rebellion.

"But the LORD sent out a great wind into the sea, and there was a mighty tempest in the sea, so that the ship was like to be broken. Then the mariners were afraid, and cried every man to his god, and cast forth the wares that were in the ship into the sea, to lighten it of them. But Jonah was gone down into the sides of the ship; and he lay, and was fast asleep. So the shipmaster came to him, and said to him, What mean you, O sleeper? Arise, call on your God, if so be that God will think on us, that we perish not. And they said every one to his fellow, Come, and let us cast lots, that we may know for whose cause this evil is on us. So they cast lots, and the lot fell on Jonah. Then said they to him, Tell us, we pray you, for whose cause this evil is on us; What is your occupation? And from where come you? What is your country? And of what people are you? And he said to them, I am an Hebrew; and I fear the LORD, the God of Heaven, which has made the sea and the dry land. Then were the men exceedingly afraid, and said to him. Why have you done this? For the men knew that he fled from the presence of the LORD, because he had told them.
Then said they to him, What shall we do to you, that the sea may be calm to us? for the sea worked, and was tempestuous. And he said to them, Take me up, and cast me

The Revelation of a Gift

forth into the sea; so shall the sea be calm to you: for I know that for my sake this great tempest is on you. Nevertheless the men rowed hard to bring it to the land; but they could not: for the sea worked, and was tempestuous against them. Why they cried to the LORD, and said, We beseech you, O LORD, we beseech you, let us not perish for this man's life, and lay not on us innocent blood: for you, O LORD, have done as it pleased you. So they look up Jonah, and cast him forth into the sea: and the sea ceased from her raging. Then the men feared the LORD exceedingly, and offered a sacrifice to the LORD, and made vows. Now the LORD had prepared a great fish to swallow up Jonah. And Jonah was in the belly of the fish three days and three nights."

Jonah 1:4-17

Jonah wasn't in a ship like his predecessor, Noah. Of course, we've heard it said that Jonah was swallowed by a whale, but the Bible doesn't specifically identify the type of fish Jonah had been swallowed by. It simply said that he'd been devoured by "a large fish." Some historians believe that he was swallowed by a now extinct marine animal, possibly a sea dragon or some other large fish. The Bible specifically mentions one such creature; it's called leviathan. Isaiah 27:1 says, "In that day, Yahweh with his hard and great and strong sword will punish leviathan, the fleeing serpent, and leviathan the twisted serpent; and he will kill the dragon that is in the sea."

Leviathan is the symbol of pride. As a matter of fact, in Job 41:34, God referenced leviathan as being the *king* of the proud. In other words, it's possible and likely that Jonah was not swallowed by a whale. Instead, he had been swallowed up by pride or, better yet, a scaly sea serpent called leviathan. Jonah was not released from the belly of the creature until he humbled himself and accepted his assignment. It was then that the creature vomited him out on dry land. (Note: 71% of the Earth is covered by water, and only five percent of the ocean has been explored. This means that 95% of the ocean has never been examined. According to scientists, 86% of the Earth's species has yet to be discovered or cataloged.)

In Jonah's previous season, he had been a man so proud that he'd chosen to disobey God, but after he found himself in the cave of his new season (the fish's belly), he'd humbled himself. (Note: In the ministry of deliverance, the leviathan spirit only comes out after the person bound by it humbles himself or herself.) The sea serpent hadn't just spit Jonah out, it humbled him before spitting him out into his next season. Jonah finally obeyed God, went to Ninevah, and cried out against it. The people of Ninevah repented and humbled themselves through fasting. Because of this, God's wrath was turned from Ninevah and the people were spared.

In the darkness of the fish's belly, Jonah had time to reflect. There was no turning back for him. Life, for Jonah, would never be normal again. He had to accept the fact that he was a prophet, and as such, he could not be bound by the many seasons of normality he'd someday enter. The fish's belly had been his cave, and while he was there, Jonah had to sit in utter darkness. This is the trench or deepest part of a cave known, once again, as the dark zone.

We don't know how long it took the sea creature to vomit Jonah out. Most of us have imagined Jonah's deliverance to be instantaneous, but this is unlikely. Instead, it is likely that this event took several minutes to several hours. Why is this important to note? Because it helps us to understand that coming out of a cave involves a process. Much like a birth canal, Jonah had to be pushed through the creature's digestive system. This was his exodus; this moment in time gave Jonah time to reflect on his old season. It also helped him to appreciate the season he was about to enter. Can you imagine the moment when he saw the light (revelation) of his next season?

Every new thing has a moment of revelation, from the smallest to the greatest. Everything that is covered has the potential to be revealed, but revelation without light (truth) is deception. Today, you'll come across many religions and groups that are full of information, but no revelation. They have knowledge, but no understanding; they have depth, but no height (spiritual stature); they have a form of godliness, but deny the power thereof. They put light for darkness and darkness for light. They are the blind who lead the blind into a ditch. Information is present for just about anyone who wants it, but only the Spirit of Truth can grant us insight (inward sight) into the mysteries of God.

Genesis 1:1-2 reads, "In the beginning God created the Heavens and the Earth. Now the Earth was formless and empty, darkness was over the surface of the deep, and the Spirit of God was hovering over the waters."

The word *hover* in this text is the Hebrew word *kathizo*, and it literally means to sit on, to tarry or to cover. So, God sat on the Earth very much like a hen sits on her eggs.

Another point to highlight is where the scripture says that the Earth was formless and empty, and darkness was over the surface of the deep. What this tells us is that darkness was already in existence, but God addressed the darkness by creating light. Genesis 1:3-5 goes on to say, "And God said, Let there be light: and there was light. And God saw the light, that it was good: and God divided the light from the darkness. And God called the light Day, and the darkness he called Night."

The Revelation of a Gift

The Greek word for *light* is *phós*, and it means to reveal or illuminate a thing. So, what we've come to understand is that God first hid or covered the Earth before He revealed its potential. Remember that the word *revelation* comes from the Greek word *apokalupsis*, which is where we get the word *apocalypse*, and it literally means to uncover or unveil.

Understand this—there is *always* darkness before there is light. Without darkness, we would not need revelation. Without darkness, we would not appreciate revelation. Our dark seasons are our seasons of ignorance. These are the times when we're trying to figure out what to do, what we're doing wrong, who we should be connected to, who we should be disconnecting from and so on. These are the times when we pray the most frustrating prayers because we're pregnant with an answer that has yet to be revealed. Eventually, the gift of revelation unveils itself, and we're able to see and understand what was once a mystery to us.

Consider the death and crucifixion of Jesus. Did the Jews who crucified Him know that He was the Son of God? No. Remember, He talked about the concealment of revelation in Matthew 13:13. "Therefore speak I to them in parables; because seeing they see not, and hearing they hear not, neither do they understand." Nevertheless, after He passed, an earthquake ensued, and it was during this earthquake that many of their eyes were opened. In other words, they were no longer walking in darkness. This was very much similar to the sobering moment when the people who'd laughed at Noah realized that he had truly heard from God.

"Now from the sixth hour <u>there was darkness</u> over all the land until the ninth hour. And about the ninth hour Jesus cried with a loud voice, saying, Eli, Eli, lama sabachthani? That is, My God, my God, why hast thou forsaken me? And some of them stood there, when they heard it, said, This

The Revelation of a Gift

man calleth Elijah. And straightway one of them ran, and took a sponge, and filled it with vinegar, and put it on a reed, and gave him to drink. And the rest said, Let be; let us see whether Elijah cometh to save him. And Jesus cried again with a loud voice, and yielded up his spirit. And behold, <u>the veil of the temple was rent</u> in two from the top to the bottom; and the earth did quake; and the rocks were rent; and the tombs were opened; and <u>many bodies of the saints that had fallen asleep were raised; and coming forth out of the tombs after his resurrection they entered into the holy city and appeared unto many</u>. **Now the centurion, and they that were with him watching Jesus, when they saw the earthquake, and the things that were done, feared exceedingly, saying, Truly this was the Son of God."**
Matthew 27:45-54

How were they able to say, "Truly, this was the Son of God?" Because the darkness lifted. The veil at the temple split and many of the dead *appeared* before them. It was in that moment that they realized they'd rejected a gift sent to them from God, wrapped in the flesh of man and filled with love. He gave us the gift of salvation, even though we are undeserving of His mercy and grace.

You are a gift. Every season in your life starts and ends with a revelation or a series of revelations. If you haven't received the revelation of your last season, it's simply because you're still in the genesis, exodus or some other chapter of that era, even if you've removed yourself from the people, plans and promises of that season. Let's revisit Exodus 14. The Jews found themselves standing face-to-face with the Red Sea. In their rear-view, they could see Pharaoh and his army coming after them. They could hear the angry yells of the Egyptians calling after them. If this wasn't terrifying enough, they found themselves standing in front of the Red Sea with no place else to turn. Death surrounded them on every side.

The Revelation of a Gift

This was their hour of darkness. Howbeit, it was at that moment that history repeated itself and a genesis took place right before their eyes. Genesis 1:9-10 reads, "And God said, Let the waters under the Heaven be gathered together to one place, and let the dry land appear: and it was so." Of course, these stories are centuries apart, but we see God moving the waters once again, but did He do this in real time? The answer is no. God is both Alpha, the Beginning, and Omega, the End. One day is like a thousand years with the Lord. What happened at the Red Sea was just God's voice breaking the sound barriers, traveling faster than the speed of light and echoing from history into their present. In other words, the victory had already been established in the history books of Heaven, and just as it had occurred when God created the Earth, Heaven and Earth began to prepare itself for yet another labor and delivery. The waters split, creating a birth canal of sorts for the Jews to pass through. Of course, the Jews had to play a major role in their own deliverance. They had to take the arduous and scary journey towards the sea's bottom and then begin their journey towards their promised land. Once they got to the other side, they had to ascend to grounds above sea level. This was their moment; this was their mountain. This was their opportunity to create an altar for the Lord and give Him thanks.

We've watched the movies made about Moses and we've seen the depictions of the Red Sea scene. In almost every movie, you'll notice that when the Red Sea splits, the Jews walked on a level plane or, in some films, the people went slightly downhill towards the sea. This is not a true depiction of that historical moment. How so? I'm sure you've heard the words *sea level* before. As of today, the Red Sea's depth varies from a little over three hundred feet in depth to well over nine thousand feet in depth. Of course, we know that God split the Red Sea well over three thousand years ago, but the sea was still deep then—it had to be. This means

The Revelation of a Gift

that they had to descend, almost like going down a mountain. This also means that to come out of the Red Sea, they had to climb upward or ascend. In other words, they had to come up to come out.

The ark had to rise above the earth. In other words, they had to elevate their thinking. They could no longer think and reason like the Egyptians they'd been enslaved by. They had to receive a new heart and a new mind. They couldn't just build a tower to Heaven, they had to humble themselves. They couldn't just come out the belly of the fish that had swallowed them, they had to obey their way out. God had given them a gift, and now, it was up to them to show their gratitude by obeying Him, serving Him and teaching their children to do the same.

In the biblical days, many of the patriarchs would build altars for God or have encounters with Him at the tops of mountains. The top or peak of a mountain represented the peak of a season; it was the moment when man had an encounter with God and received the revelation he needed to move forward. It represented ascension, not just in the natural, but in the realm of the spirit. In other words, the patriarch had been upgraded or elevated; it means that he'd received a promotion. He wasn't just promoted by title, he was promoted in rank. Again, he had to come up to come out. He had to come out of normality; he had to forsake his own plans and embrace the call of God on his life.

If you've ever witnessed someone going through deliverance, you've likely heard the minister say to the malevolent spirit in that person, "Come up and come out!" This means that the spirit is in the depths of that person's being; it's in a dark place. To come up isn't a directional term in the spirit realm; it means to come out of the darkness (low place) and into the marvelous light of revelation. The minister is literally telling the evil spirit to reveal itself, reveal its purpose, reveal its legal grounds and to come out in the open to be judged. Some ministers don't use the term "up and out." Instead, they simply say, "Go to the feet of Jesus." In this, they are essentially giving the malevolent force the same command; they are calling it out of its hiding place and sending it where it cannot hide and it cannot stand (because it must bow)—they are sending it to the Judgment Seat of God. This is their exodus, only, they are spiritual troglobites; they have been in darkness for so long that they have no eyes to see. Simply put, they cannot comprehend light (revelation). Note: this is why Jesus hides wisdom in parables.

You are a gift, and as such, you have to be delivered to the person or people God has designed you to bless. All the same, you have to be delivered from some of the people, plans and situations that you've delivered yourself to. You are the answer to somebody's prayers, but it's hard for you to know this when you're in the caves of normality trying to make a name for yourself. The journey isn't about delivering the stuff that you want; the real journey is about deliverance —it's about getting you to birth out your potential. Of course, this won't happen until you first understand that *you are a gift*. It doesn't matter what you've done or where you are in your walk with Christ, you are the answer to someone's prayer. Romans 8:19 says it this way, "For the earnest expectation of the creature waits for the manifestation of the sons of God." Other translations use the word *revealing*, instead of *manifestation*. In other words, Heaven and Earth are waiting for *you* to find out who you are! Before the Jews could be delivered from under the oppressive thumb of Pharaoh, they had to wait for Moses to realize who he was! Moses left Egypt and moved to Midian after he went into exile. There, he worked as a shepherd for his father-in-law, Jethro, for forty years before returning to set the captives free. Moses had been a gift to the Jews, but they hadn't initially recognized this fact or received him as such. They likely saw him as entitled, privileged and unable to empathize with their plight. He was a gift to God's people, but he'd revealed himself too soon. So, he went away to Midian.

Why did Moses flee to Midian in the first place? Exodus 2:11-15 tells the story. "And it came to pass in those days, when Moses was grown, that he went out to his brothers, and looked on their burdens: and he spied an Egyptian smiting an Hebrew, one of his brothers. And he looked this way and that way, and when he saw that there was no man, he slew the Egyptian, and hid him in the sand. And when he went out the second day, behold, two men of the Hebrews strove together: and he said to him that did the wrong, Why smite you your fellow? And he said, Who made you a prince and a judge over us? intend you to kill me, as you killed the Egyptian? And Moses feared, and said, Surely this thing is known. Now when Pharaoh heard this thing, he sought to slay Moses. But Moses fled from the face of Pharaoh, and dwelled in the land of Midian: and he sat down by a well."

When Elijah had been threatened by Jezebel, he'd run and hid himself in a cave, but as we can see, Elijah hadn't been the first man to run from a wicked ruler. David had done the same, and here, we can see that Moses was the very first man mentioned in the Bible to do this. However, Moses had not hid himself in a physical cave; he'd hid himself in a metaphorical cave. Midian, for Moses, was his cave, and he dwelt there for forty years. And it was in Midian that God trained Moses for his next role. He'd gone from being the adopted grandson of Pharaoh to a shepherd leading and cleaning up behind his father-in-law's sheep. And we can safely assume that after forty years, Moses had become comfortable in his new role. He probably thought he'd live out the rest of his years chasing away wolves and cleaning up dung, and he was right—just not in the way he'd imagined. He had to leave his cave and return to Egypt. His cave represented a place of refuge, a place of comfort and a dwelling place, but if he had not answered the call on his life, his cave could have easily become his final resting place. In his cave, Moses had to allow his father-in-law to unbox his potential. He'd sent Moses out into the field, making him a shepherd. He had to return to the valley that was Egypt in order to help his brethren ascend out of their bondage. He returned to Egypt as a gift to God's people. He left his job as a sheep-herder or shepherd to answer the call on his life. The forty years he'd spent in Midian had been instrumental in developing him for his next role. Moses had been a gift to his father-in-law, Jethro, and it was for this reason that Jethro gave him his daughter, Zipporah. She was Moses's gift, but he could not fully give himself to her. He couldn't surrender to a life of normality. He had so much more potential that was scheduled to be unpacked. So, God sent Moses back to Egypt to be the gift He'd designed him to be. He became a gift to the Israelites, demanding that Pharaoh set God's people free. After Pharaoh and his army had been destroyed, Moses was the gift that led God's people through the wilderness towards the promised land. But because of their hard hearts, Moses was unable to lead them into the promised land. Another gift from God by the name of Joshua had to finish up that assignment.

So, what can we take from all these stories? What have you learned about the revelation of a gift? A few important pointers are:
1. **God wants to build history with you.** When God delivered the Jews from Egypt, He would often remind them that He is the God who brought them out of Egypt. He was establishing history with them so that they could trust Him with their future. He

wants to do the same with you.
2. **God wants to establish trust with you.** Trust is the wiring that establishes a connection between us and God. Trust in God is faith in God; it's our soul tie or how we tie our soul to Him.
3. **God wants to personally walk and talk with you.** Can two walk together except they be agreed? God desires to have an intimate relationship with you so that He can share His heart with you.
4. **God wants to develop you.** This means that the Lord wants to mature you. Development involves a process, but the end-goal is getting you to stand firm on His Word so that He can use you to develop others.
5. **God wants you to humble yourself.** Humility is the sweet perfume that attracts the favor of God.
6. **God wants to deliver you.** God delivered Noah and his family from the impending flood. God delivered the Jews from Egypt. God delivered Jonah from the belly of the great fish. When we're free, we get to experience God in a way that we couldn't have experienced Him if we had remained bound. For this reason, God specializes in deliverance.
7. **God wants to reveal Himself to you and through you.** Matthew 6:33 reads, "But seek ye first the kingdom of God, and his righteousness; and all these things shall be added unto you." The Kingdom of God is the heart of God. God wants to reveal Himself to you so that you'll trust Him enough to let Him reveal Himself through you.

Every story of deliverance ends in revelation. As a gift of God and a gift from God, it is important that you understand how to navigate the season you're in. Understand that every season has a start and every season has an end. In every season, you have to ascend and you

The Revelation of a Gift

have to descend. One of the evidences that a season has come or is coming to an end is when that season reaches the height of normality and becomes a comfort zone. Believe it or not, Egypt had become a place of comfort for the Jews. Yes, they'd prayed and complained about their circumstances, but they'd also grown accustomed to them.

Gifts are revealed over time. Gifts are revealed in certain seasons. Gifts are revealed to certain people. Gifts are transferred or delivered from one reality to the next until they find themselves in the right hands. Gifts can be stolen, but the thief cannot unravel the gift. He can only utilize what has already been uncovered. As a gift, it is important for you to understand that every cave season is just an opportunity for God to prepare you for the next season. God will intentionally hide your value from the wrong people; this is so that their inability to see your worth will frustrate you until you remove yourself from them. This process will repeat itself until the fullness of who you are is on display. By this time, you'll be in a high place, and the only people who'll be able to reach you are the people who God has given eyes to see and ears to hear.

In summary, you may be feeling impatient, invaluable and insignificant, but please understand that God is strategic and intentional regarding you. Every small and large event that you have encountered or are in the midst of encountering may very well be the training grounds for your next assignment. Don't allow impatience or rejection to drive you out of your cave prematurely. If Noah hadn't waited for all of the instructions to build the ark, it is possible that he would have built the very first submarine to ever exist. If Jonah had tried to fight his way out of the fish's belly, instead of repenting and waiting for his next set of instructions, it is possible that he could have ended up as dung at the bottom of the sea. If Moses hadn't come back to

Egypt to confront Pharaoh, God would have had to raise up another deliverer for His people. The point is, your wait and your process both have purpose. You may not see yourself as a mighty deliverer of God's people, but this won't stop God from using you howsoever He chooses to use you. Let God, through time, unwrap and unbox your potential. Your job is to simply stay in the will of God, listen for the voice of God and follow His instructions. He'll take it from there.

See Depths of a Cave Diagram (Page 253)

MOUNTAINS OF INFLUENCE

"And there came one of the seven angels that had the seven bowls, and spake with me, saying, Come hither, I will show thee the judgment of the great harlot that sitteth upon many waters; with whom the kings of the Earth committed fornication, and they that dwell in the Earth were made drunken with the wine of her fornication. And he carried me away in the Spirit into a wilderness: and I saw a woman sitting upon a scarlet-colored beast, full of names of blasphemy, having seven heads and ten horns. And the woman was arrayed in purple and scarlet, and decked with gold and precious stone and pearls, having in her hand a golden cup full of abominations, even the unclean things of her fornication, and upon her forehead a name written, MYSTERY, BABYLON THE GREAT, THE MOTHER OF THE HARLOTS AND OF THE ABOMINATIONS OF THE EARTH. And I saw the woman drunken with the blood of the saints, and with the blood of the martyrs of Jesus. And when I saw her, I wondered with a great wonder.
And the angel said unto me, Wherefore didst thou wonder? I will tell thee the mystery of the woman, and of the beast that carrieth her, which hath the seven heads and the ten horns. The beast that thou sawest was, and is not; and is about to come up out of the abyss, and to go into perdition. And they that dwell on the earth shall wonder, they whose name hath not been written in the book of life from the foundation of the world, when they behold the beast, how that he was, and is not, and shall come. Here is the mind that hath wisdom. The seven heads are seven mountains, on which the woman

sitteth: and they are seven kings; the five are fallen, the one is, the other is not yet come; and when he cometh, he must continue a little while. And the beast that was, and is not, is himself also an eighth, and is of the seven; and he goeth into perdition."

Revelation 17:1-11

Most of us have heard of the seven mountains of influence. If you have not, they are:
- Religion
- Family
- Education
- Government
- Media
- Arts & Entertainment
- Business

In Revelation 17, the Apostle John is detailing a vision he had seen. He saw a woman sitting on a scarlet-colored, seven-headed beast. The angel that was with him explained that the seven heads represent seven mountains and seven kings. Of course, every king has a kingdom. In short, the seven mountains referenced here are the seven mountains of influence.

The first record of the Seven Mountain Mandate can be traced back to the year 1975. Bill Bright, the founder of Campus Crusade, was having lunch with Loren Cunningham, the founder of Youth with a Mission. Both men had a dream that they wanted to share with one another—a dream that had been given to them by God. Around that same time, an American Evangelical Christian, Presbyterian Pastor and theologian by the name of Francis Schaeffer was also teaching and studying the same revelation. All three men believed and taught that in order for the church to effectively have dominion, we need to influence and gain dominion over the seven mountains of influence. Before we go any further, let's scale back a little so that we can better understand how this revelation affects us.

What is a cave? Let's revisit the definition. Merriam Webster defines the word *cave* three ways:
1. a natural chamber or series of chambers in the earth or in the side of a hill or cliff
2. usually an underground chamber for storage
3. a place providing privacy or seclusion from others

The definition we want to focus on in this presentation is, "a natural chamber or series of chambers in the earth or in the side of a hill or cliff." In short, caves can be found:
1. in the earth (these are dens that go underground)
2. in the sides of mountains
3. in the side of cliffs

As climbers ascend mountains, they are often met with storms, weariness and disease. When this happens, they can find refuge in a cave. Of course, the goal is to reach the summit or peak of that mountain, but climbers understand that in order for this to happen, they have to be physically and emotionally healthy. In the United States, there are some mountains that must be ascended with the aid of a guide, while others can be attempted without a guide. Less than fifty percent of the people who ascend mountains have actually ever reached the top of a mountain. This is because the air is thinner at the top of each mountain, thus, making it harder for the climber to breathe. Additionally, inexperience, weather conditions and poor planning all play a role in this statistic. Nevertheless, the men and women who've successfully reached the summit of a mountain can tell you that they had to take strategic moments just to rest. It was during these moments that they looked for dens or caves to retreat into.

The Apprenticeship Model: A Journey Towards Mastery is an article penned by Dr. Christopher Perrin and published on Classical Academics Press. In his article, Dr. Perrin detailed three levels to mastery, and with each level, there were ranks. The chart he published is below.

Level 1	Level 2	Level 3
Apprentice	Journeyman	Master
Assistant	Associate	Mentor/Master
Beginner	Advanced	Expert
Learner	Practitioner	Trainer

(Source: Classical Academic Press/The Apprenticeship Model: A Journey toward Mastery/ Dr. Christopher Perrin)

According to this chart, we have to ascend Level One; this is our first mountain. Here, we go from Learner to Beginner to Assistant, and we finally arrive at Apprentice. From here, we start a new season, but in this particular season, we are at the bottom once again. Now, we are on Level Two, and we start this level as a Practitioner. We have to climb this mountain for several years before we reach Level Three. Once we reach Level Three, we are right back at the bottom again. We've gone from being at the top of our game to becoming a rookie yet again. This is why we have to remain humble. On Level Three, we start off as a Trainer, and we have to climb that mountain until we've become a Master.

In the Learner stage of Level One, there are caves, just as there are caves on the Mentor/Master of Level Three. As we're climbing towards the top of the Learner's level, we will find ourselves needing to rest and recalibrate. If we want to reach the top of this level and go on to the next level, we have to utilize these caves.

Now, let's apply this chart to the seven mountains of influence. God has called each of us to one or more of these mountains, even if we aren't called to the top of any of them. Just like a natural mountain, there are levels on the mountains of influence, and sadly enough, the enemy has been dominating each mountain. Satan has strategically placed his children throughout each plane in Religion, Family, Education, Government, Media, Arts & Entertainment and Business. At the same time, he's placed his children at the top of these mountains. This isn't because he's powerful, after all, Jesus stripped him of his power close to two millenniums ago; that's close to two thousand years ago. Satan borrows or steals his power from the people who God entrusted power with—God's children. He robs us of this power through fear, ambition, temptation, frustration, offense and any other weapon he can form against us. But how does Satan get his children on each of these levels? Through a system called *sacrifice*. When a man in the entertainment industry decides that he wants to grow his career, he must make a series of sacrifices. And while he may not shed any blood, he's using his blood, sweat and tears to reach his goal. His family also pays for his ambition. If he climbs the ranks without God, Satan will require more from him before each promotion. "And to whomsoever much is given, of him shall much be required: and to whom they commit much, of him will they ask the more" (Luke 12:48). It's no secret in the music industry that many of the men and women at the top have denounced God, made pledges with demons and committed violent acts just to ascend the Mountain of Arts & Entertainment. This is why Apostle Mark said in Mark 8:36, "For what shall it profit a man, if he shall gain the whole world, and lose his own soul?"

As you ascend the ranks of this thing we call life, and as you ascend the mountain or mountains of influence that God has assigned you to, it is important for you to remember that you have to ascend each level, but as you ascend, God will strategically call you into a cave. Maybe your realm of influence is family. If this is so, you may have found that your family has been under attack for a long time. Generation after generation, they've fought one another, and for this reason, your family has been severely divided for a long time. Hear me—to combat this, you have to pray, fast and fight for your family, not against them! The enemy knows that your family has the potential to disrupt his plans on the Mountain of Family, and of course, he does not want this to happen. Sometimes, we have to go and clean up the messes our parents, grandparents and even our ancestors have left behind! But to do this, we must humble ourselves and be led by the Spirit of God. And remember, God doesn't always lead us to where we want to go. Sometimes, He will lead us into the wilderness. The wilderness is just another cave. Matthew 4:1 confirms this. It states, "Then was Jesus led up of the spirit into the wilderness to be tempted of the devil." Apostle John had a similar encounter. Revelation 17:1-3 reads, ""And there came one of the seven angels that had the seven bowls, and spake with me, saying, Come hither, I will show thee the judgment of the great harlot that sitteth upon many waters; with whom the kings of the Earth committed fornication, and they that dwell in the Earth were made drunken with the wine of her fornication. And he carried me away in the Spirit into a wilderness."

The point is, in order to ascend the mountains of influence, you have to be willing to have your plans disrupted by God. And you have to be humble enough to start at the bottom after you've spent time at the top. Again, more than fifty percent of climbers never reach the top of the mountains they've ascended. Sadly enough, this figure may be lower for believers ascending the mountains of influence. This is because most believers lack the information and the support they need to climb. Remember what God said when the people of the earth were trying to build the Tower of Babel. He said, "Behold, they are one people, and they have all one language; and this is what they begin to do: and now nothing will be withholden from them, which they purpose to do" (Genesis 11:6). Unity shortens the distance and the time between one season to another. It is then no wonder that the enemy works diligently to get Christians, churches and denominations to be at war with one another.

Lastly, each cave along the side of a mountain represents a season. In other words, it is not the will of God for you to become too comfortable in whatever cave you're in. One of the signs that you're getting too comfortable in a place is when you start purchasing furniture for it, hanging pictures on the wall, moving stuff around and receiving mail. When God sees this, He will often disrupt our caves by allowing the storms of life to knock over our plans and short-circuit our relationships. It would be foolish for you to curse God or curse your season should this happen. He's simply ensuring that you'll be able to transition to the next season seamlessly. There are many gifts out there who have gotten stuck in transition. This is because they were in the valley somewhere between Egypt and their promised land complaining and reminiscing, instead of moving forward.

HOW TO HANDLE BEING HIDDEN

"It is the glory of God to conceal a thing: but the honour of kings is to search out a matter."
Proverbs 25:2

First off, let's look at the etymology of the word glory.

"c. 1200, gloire "the splendor of God or Christ; praise offered to God, worship," from Old French glorie "glory (of God); worldly honor, renown; splendor, magnificence, pomp" (11c., Modern French gloire), from Latin gloria "fame, renown, great praise or honor," a word of uncertain origin.

> The etymology as *gnoria "knowledge, fame" to gnarus "known" and i-gnorare has been acknowledged by some scholars, and rejected by others. In its favour speak the semantics of words for "glory", which in Indo-European societies mostly have to do with "spoken praise", 'reputation by hearsay'. Against the assumed etymology speak the phonetics. [de Vaan]

Meaning 'one who is a source of glory' is from mid-14c. Also, in Middle English 'thirst for glory, vainglory, pride, boasting, vanity' (late 14c.), Sense of 'magnificence' is late 14c. in English. Meaning "worldly honor, fame, renown.' Latin also had gloriola 'a little fame.' Glory days was in use by 1970. Old Glory for 'the American flag' is first attested 1862.

How to Handle Being Hidden

The Christian sense are from the Latin word's use in the Bible to translate Greek doxa 'expectation' (Homer), later 'an opinion, judgment," and later still 'opinion others have of one (good or bad), fame; glory,' which was used in Biblical writing to translate a Hebrew word which had a sense of 'brightness, splendor, magnificence, majesty of outward appearance.' The religious use has colored that word's meaning in most European tongues. Wuldor was an Old English word used in this sense
mid-14c., 'to rejoice' (now always with in), from Old French gloriier 'glorify; pride oneself on, boast about,' and directly from Latin gloriari which in classical use meant 'to boast, vaunt, brag, pride oneself,' from gloria (see glory (n.) Related: Gloried; glorying."
(Source: Online Etymology Dictionary/ Glory)

So, what exactly does the scripture mean when it says it is the glory of God to conceal a thing? It means that hiding you, hiding your gifts and hiding your potential is God's pride and joy. If you're a parent, you can probably understand how exciting it is to box up and wrap gifts for your children, especially if those boxes contain gifts that your children have been asking for or gifts you know they'll cherish. So, when God hid your potential and boxed up your identity, He did this with pride and joy. When that man or woman couldn't figure you out, God beamed with joy because He'd wrapped you well. The enemy has sent many people into your life disguising themselves as friends, but even when you opened yourself up to these people, God still hid the mystery that is you from them. They could see your present state, but they couldn't see your future. They could see snippets of your potential, but what little they did see wasn't enough to help them understand just how valuable you are. That's because you are a walking, talking parable. Again, you're like a diamond on a secluded island. Let's revisit the story about the diamond and the coconut.

You can feel the warmth of the man's hands who's just picked you up. Maybe this time, someone will see just how valuable you are. But all of a sudden, the man draws back and throws you with all of his might towards a tree. Upon impact, you realize that you've hit a coconut. The coconut falls out of the tree and doesn't land too far from where you've landed. The hungry man then walks past you and picks up the coconut. You're frustrated because on that island, no one seems to know your worth, despite how much you shine.

But one day, you see the residents of the island pointing towards a ship on the horizon. This ship belongs to the United States Navy and it's been deployed to help find the person who's been shipwrecked on the island. Upon being rescued, he decides to grab every diamond, ruby and jewel that he could find since the island's residents don't value them. The natives of the island wave in delight as the ship sets sail, heading back to America. (Remember, in this scenario, you are the diamond.) Once you're appraised, the appraiser determines that you're worth 75 billion dollars, and only the infamous one percent of the world's elite can afford you. Before long, you're in a museum on display, and everyone stops to admire your luster. Your season of concealment wasn't as short-lived as you would have liked it to be, but had you been found just five or ten years earlier, you wouldn't have been appraised for half of what you've been appraised for now. The point is, God is hiding you, your value and your potential for the right people at the right time in the right place. This is why long-suffering, which is just another word for patience, is one of the fruits of the Holy Spirit.

One of the strengths and weaknesses of a gift can be summarized by a single word: adaptation. Because of His ingenuity, God gave us all the innate ability to adapt to some of the harshest conditions. This is a survival mechanism that He's gifted us with. While Darwin's theory of evolution is false, it does contain some grains of truth. In Darwin's theory, a bear's descendants could evolve into a family of whales if they spent the majority of their lives in water generation after generation. This is a creative lie and a misrepresentation of true scientific research. In other words, it's an assumption that was published as a fact, even though there is little to no evidence supporting it. In short, Darwin's theory suggests that, for example, a species of animals could possibly evolve into a completely different and distinctive species if placed in environments that are not conducive to their survival. A monkey cannot evolve into a human; we know this because science has proven it! Nevertheless, a human's features can and does change over time to increase the likelihood of survival. Check out the following article from SciMex regarding the shape of the human nose: "The size and shape of the nose in different human populations is not simply the result of chance, but evolved, at least in part, in response to local climate conditions, report Arslan Zaidi and Mark Shriver of Pennsylvania State University, in a study published March 16th, 2017, in *PLOS Genetics*.

The nose is one of humanity's most distinctive facial features, which also has the important job of conditioning the air that we breathe, to ensure that it is warm and moist when it reaches the lungs, which helps to prevent infections. Previous studies suggest that people whose ancestors lived in hot, humid places tend to have wider nostrils than people whose ancestors came from cold and dry environments, but whether these differences arose in response to local climates or just due to chance was unknown. In the current study, researchers examined the size and shape of noses on people with West African, South Asian, East Asian, or Northern European ancestry and found that differences in nose shape across these populations are greater than can be explained by chance alone. Additionally, wider nostrils are correlated with ancestors who evolved in warmer temperatures and with greater absolute humidity, suggesting that climate was one factor driving nasal evolution. The nose has had a complex evolutionary history, however, and researchers suspect that additional factors, such as cultural preferences when picking a mate, have also played a role in shaping the nose.

Investigations into nose shape evolution and climate adaptation may have medical as well as anthropological implications. Studies of human adaptation are essential to our understanding of disease and yield insights into why certain conditions, such as sickle cell anemia, lactose intolerance or skin cancer, are more common in certain populations. The researchers suggest that it may be worth investigating whether the shape of the nose and the size of the nasal cavity impact one's risk of contracting a respiratory disease when living in a climate that is different from one's ancestors.

Arslan A. Zaidi adds: 'Even though there are substantial differences in nose shape among human populations, much of this variation can be explained by random genetic drift alone. This finding is in line with the consensus that most human variation is shared among populations and primarily due to genetic drift. Traits like skin pigmentation and nostril width are exceptions rather than the rule. Having said that, these traits are important to study because they are likely tied to our health, especially as we become more of a global community and migrate to new climes.'"
(Source: SciMex/Hot or cold, climate helped shape your nose/PLOS Genetics)

In short, our bodies do evolve, but our humanity doesn't. We won't eventually become mountain lions if we start living in the clefts of mountains. Again, there is a survival mechanism in all of us that allows us to adapt to our conditions. This is why a woman can be sex trafficked—she can be mentally, physically and sexually abused, and have absolutely no desire to leave her lifestyle. After all, she's adapted to the lifestyle she's leading. To everyone outside of her world, she needs to be rescued, and while this is true, it is important that she first realizes this. Otherwise, she'll return to that world every time someone takes her out of it.

As a gift, God will repeatedly place you in seasons of obscurity, but it is your responsibility to make sure that you're getting the development, love and encouragement you need in those seasons. It is also your responsibility to ensure that you don't grow so accustomed to obscurity that you start unpacking your fears, doubts and plans, and using them as furniture for your cave. You'd be amazed at the number of gifts who've allowed their wombs to become their tombs. You'd be amazed if you knew the number of five-fold gifts that have never touched a mic, cast out a devil or interceded for someone. They have adapted to their caves and become slaves of normality. They worked in fields that they hated and stood by passively as their health decreased, nevertheless, they refused to embrace the calls on their lives. Their caves became the great fishes that swallowed them whole, however, unlike Jonah, they didn't repent, so they were never spit out of their caves. Instead, they lived, adapted to and died in obscurity. Again, this is why Dr. Myles Munroe's quote was so priceless. Just to reiterate, Mr. Munroe said, "The wealthiest place on the planet is just down the road. It is the cemetery. There lie buried companies that were never started, inventions that were never made, bestselling books that were never written, and masterpieces that were never painted. In the cemetery is buried the greatest treasure of untapped potential."

In the cemetery, there are prophets who've never prophesied, evangelists who've never won a soul for Christ, pastors who've never shepherded, teachers who've never taught, and apostles who've never exercised any measure of their God-given authority. These are buried gifts. Elisha received a double-portion anointing from Elijah, but he never passed the mantle. For this reason, he died with his potential locked up inside him. 2 Kings 13:20-21 tells a pretty interesting story. It reads, "And Elisha died, and they buried him. Now the bands of the Moabites invaded the land at the coming in of the year. And it came to pass, as they were burying a man, that, behold, they spied a band; and they cast the man into the sepulchre of Elisha: and as soon as the man touched the bones of Elisha, he revived, and stood up on his feet."

This story alone is the catalyst behind the emerging and demonic craze that is known as grave soaking (also known as grave sucking and mantle grabbing). This necromantic practice involves people going to the graves of preachers and evangelists and laying across those graves in an attempt to soak up or absorb the person's anointing. The problem behind this is, God specifically forbids necromancy or any practice that resembles it, plus, there are living, breathing anointed people all around us. They are in churches, nursing homes, prisons and pretty much everywhere you look. Why not just go and sit at their feet, as opposed to laying on their graves once they're dead and gone? The simple answer is, they lack the love needed to inconvenience themselves for others. They'd rather lay on a dead man's grave than to be tasked with the responsibility of visiting or encouraging that same man when he is alive and in need. The point is, don't bury your gifts and don't bury yourself in caves, otherwise, you run the risk of becoming the unfaithful servant who buried his talents. Let's revisit the parable.

"For the kingdom of Heaven is as a man traveling into a far country, who called his own servants, and delivered to them his goods. And to one he gave five talents, to another two, and to another one; to every man according to his several ability; and straightway took his journey. Then he that had received the five talents went and traded with the same, and made them other five talents. And likewise he that had received two, he also gained other two. But he that had received one went and dig in the earth, and hid his lord's money.

After a long time the lord of those servants comes, and reckons with them. And so he that had received five talents came and brought other five talents, saying, Lord, you delivered to me five talents: behold, I have gained beside them five talents more. His lord said to him, Well done, you good and faithful servant: you have been faithful over a few things, I will make you ruler over many things: enter you into the joy of your lord.

He also that had received two talents came and said, Lord, you delivered to me two talents: behold, I have gained two other talents beside them. His lord said to him, Well done, good and faithful servant; you have been faithful over a few things, I will make you ruler over many things: enter you into the joy of your lord.

Then he which had received the one talent came and said, Lord, I knew you that you are an hard man, reaping where you have not sown, and gathering where you have not strewed: And I was afraid, and went and hid your talent in the earth: see, there you have that is yours.

His lord answered and said to him, You wicked and slothful servant, you knew that I reap where I sowed not, and gather where I have not strewed: You ought therefore to have put my money to the exchangers, and then at my coming I should have received my own with usury. Take therefore the talent from him, and give it to him which has ten talents."

Matthew 25:14-28

The unfaithful servant buried his gift. He didn't sow it into good ground, he buried it. What if I told you that he was the gift he'd buried? How so? The story in itself is a parable, meaning, it's not literal. Where do we bury things? In dirt, of course. Dirt, in the scriptures, represents flesh, since we were created from the dust of the ground. The master who went away to a far country is a representation of Jesus Christ, the Bridegroom. He called his servants together and gave them all according to their several-ability, meaning, He gave them what they could bear—nothing more, nothing less. We can take this parable and explain it with another revelatory parable. Here's the extraction: to the apostle, He gave five gifts (the apostolic, prophetic, evangelistic, pastoral and the teacher's mantle). To the pastor, He gave two gifts (the office of an overseer and a wife). To the teacher, He gave one gift—the ability to teach, but the problem with the teacher was, he was supposed to remove the beam from his own eye before he would be allowed to multiply his gift. This task proved too arduous for him, so he decided to exchange his gift of teaching for a life of normality.

One day, each man died and stood before the Lord. The apostle said, "Lord, I reproduced myself, and now, there are ten churches that I've established, and they are all running well!" The Lord looked at him and said, "Well done, good and faithful servant! I will add to what you've already done, so I'm going to bless your children and their children up to twenty generations. Enter now into the rest of the Lord." The second man came forth and said, "Lord, I also reproduced myself. My wife and I ministered to others through our marriage. We even counseled others, and when we were tempted to quit on one another, we would renew our vows. For this reason, four couples who were about to get a divorce decided to stay together, and now, they are helping others do the same!" The Lord looked at the man and said, "Well done my good and faithful servant! Because of what you've done, I'm going to bless your children up to eight generations, so that divorce will never come near the thresholds of their homes or their hearts. All the same, their marriages will help to save other marriages. Enter now into my rest!" Finally, the unfaithful servant came forth. In his hand, he was carrying a book of knowledge that the Lord had placed in his belly. He handed the book back to the Lord and said, "Look, I didn't trust you because I felt like you were a God who unfairly reaped what you had not sown, and gathered what you had not scattered. But look, at least I didn't lose the gift you gave me, after all, the gifts and callings are without repentance. So, here's your gift back." The Lord looked at the false servant, judged him and sent him into utter darkness; He sent him into the dark zone.

Revelation is the unveiling or unraveling of a mystery. The story detailed in Matthew 25:14-28 has so much meat to it, and if you have an intimate relationship with the Lord, He will give you insight that goes beyond what you see spelled out on a page.

There are seasons when the Lord will call you to Himself, either physically or mentally. What do these seasons look like? When the Lord withdraws you physically, He's also withdrawing you mentally as well, but during this cave season, His focus is on spending quality time with you. So, in this season, you won't receive many visitors or phone calls, and you may find yourself feeling like you just want to be by yourself for a while. Maybe you've been having an overwhelming desire to go on a trip by yourself, or maybe you just want to take some time off work and just lock yourself in your house. Hear me—this is okay as long as you remain accountable with your feelings and your intentions. You have to make sure that you're not being driven into a cave by the spirits of fear, rejection, offense or isolation. If you believe the Lord is calling you to Himself, it is best to fast during that time and take notes detailing your thought processes and your feelings. This is similar to hibernation and torpor.

In the animal kingdom, there is hibernation and then there is torpor. The two, although similar, are not one and the same.
Hibernation: "The condition or period of an animal or plant spending the winter in a dormant state" (Source: Oxford Dictionaries).
Torpor: "A state of physical or mental inactivity; lethargy" (Source: Oxford Dictionaries).

The difference is, in hibernation, the animal enters a dormant state, whereas, it will not wake up if touched or regardless of what's going on around it. In the state of torpor, however, animals will awaken if they hear a noise or if they are touched. Additionally, they will occasionally and temporarily leave their dens. Of course, they won't be gone away from their dens for too long or go too far from their dens because their heart rate is slow during this period. So, while we often say that black bears, grizzly bears and brown bears go into hibernation, this is not entirely true. These members of the Ursidae family go into a state of tupor, but they are known to occasionally leave their dens for short periods of time. Many scientists refer to these denning periods as *winter lethargy* or *winter sleep*. While some scientists still use the term hibernation when referencing the suspended animation of a bear during the winter months, the politically correct term is tupor. Bears remain in this state for seven and a half months! True hibernators, however, include bats, chipmunks, groundhogs, turtles, bees, snakes, skunks and so on.

Before hibernation and tupor, the animal must prepare itself for its next season. Most animals will eat as much as possible so they can have fat reserves to live off of while they rest.

During hibernation, the body temperature of the resting animal goes down. Of course, just how far the temperature drops depends on the animal. Some animals, like squirrels, have temperatures that drop almost to freezing! The animal's heart rate slows down, its blood vessels constrict and their shivering reflex is suppressed to ensure that they don't burn off all their fat reserves. They have to preserve as much energy as they can, otherwise, they'll burn off all their fat prematurely and die. Some animals do wake up during hibernation to expel waste and to prevent their muscles from going into atrophy by moving around a little. Of course, they will eat or drink if they need to.

Next, there are times when you have to work and you can't break away physically. It is during these times that God may call you into a cave mentally. What does this look like? Anytime you are in a public place, whether it be at work, church or at a family gathering, you may feel disconnected from the conversations going on around you. You may find yourself looking for corners to retreat to, in hopes that no one will notice or approach you. Again, this is okay, just as long as you are accountable with your feelings and intentions.

Just like animals hibernate or going into states of torpor, we have to sometimes withdraw ourselves from the hustle and bustle of life so that we can spend time with God. We have to spend time evaluating ourselves and the seasons we're in, otherwise, we run the risk of becoming mechanical and predictable in everything that we do. If God withdraws you wholly (physically and mentally), He may be calling you to a season of total rest or He may be hiding you. If He withdraws you mentally, He may be utilizing the season you're in to develop you, for example, He may be sharpening your discernment or teaching you how to be a watchman on the wall.

How does one handle being hidden? It's absolutely necessary that we ask and answer this question because the church is losing a lot of potentially great men and women of God who, quite frankly, have never been taught how to handle obscurity. Many of them are left to believe that there's something wrong with them, and for this reason, suicide rates amongst church clergy is at an all-time high. Below are a few caves that you may find yourself in.

#1 The Cave of Bondage

"Jesus therefore again groaning in himself cometh to the tomb. Now it was a cave, and a stone lay against it. Jesus saith, Take ye away the stone. Martha, the sister of him that was dead, saith unto him, Lord, by this time the body decayeth; for he hath been dead four days. Jesus saith unto her, Said I not unto thee, that, if thou believedst, thou shouldest see the glory of God? So they took away the stone. And Jesus lifted up his eyes, and said, Father, I thank thee that thou heardest me. And I knew that thou hearest me always: but because of the multitude that standeth around I said it, that they may believe that thou didst send me. And when he had thus spoken, he cried with a loud voice, Lazarus, come forth. He that was dead came forth, bound hand and foot with grave-clothes; and his face was bound about with a napkin. Jesus saith unto them, Loose him, and let him go."

John 11:38-44

The Bible doesn't tell us much about Lazarus, except that he was the brother of Mary and Martha. Lazarus had been in his cave for four days; he was dead, and the Bible tells us that this was for the glory of God. Again, we can extract all the obvious facts from this story, or we can pull divine revelation from it. According to the story, Mary and Martha had sent for Jesus when their brother, Lazarus, was dying. Nevertheless, Jesus didn't come fast enough to save his life.

John 11:1-4 reads, "Now a certain man was sick, Lazarus of Bethany, of the village of Mary and her sister Martha. And it was that Mary who anointed the Lord with ointment, and wiped his feet with her hair, whose brother Lazarus was sick. The sisters therefore sent unto him, saying, Lord, behold, he whom thou lovest is sick. But when Jesus heard it, he said, This sickness is not unto death, but for the glory of God, that the Son of God may be glorified thereby." Needless to say, Lazarus died, but the Lord resurrected him. What can we extract from this story?

Sometimes, the Lord will allow us to go into caves for reasons far beyond our control. These are not caves that we enter to spend time with the Lord; these are seasons where God will strategically separate us from our desires so that we can die to ourselves. When we finally surrender to His will, He'll come along and roll away our stony hearts and give us a new heart and a new mind. From there, He'll remove our grave clothes and send us forth into ministry. Note: Grave clothes represent the flesh. Sure, He won't literally strip our flesh from our bones; what He does is cause us to rise above our desires so that we can fulfill His call on our lives.

This season is all about surrender.

#2 The Cave of Surrender

"And Jehovah said, I have pardoned according to thy word: but in very deed, as I live, and as all the Earth shall be filled with the glory of Jehovah; because all those men that have seen my glory, and my signs, which I wrought in Egypt and in the wilderness, yet have tempted me these ten times, and have not hearkened to my voice; surely they shall not see the land which I sware unto their fathers, neither shall any of them that despised me see it: but my servant Caleb, because he had another spirit with him, and hath followed me fully,

him will I bring into the land whereinto he went; and his seed shall possess it. Now the Amalekite and the Canaanite dwell in the valley: to-morrow turn ye, and get you into the wilderness by the way to the Red Sea.
And Jehovah spake unto Moses and unto Aaron, saying, How long shall I bear with this evil congregation, that murmur against me? I have heard the murmurings of the children of Israel, which they murmur against me. Say unto them, As I live, saith Jehovah, surely as ye have spoken in mine ears, so will I do to you: your dead bodies shall fall in this wilderness; and all that were numbered of you, according to your whole number, from twenty years old and upward, that have murmured against me, surely ye shall not come into the land, concerning which I sware that I would make you dwell therein, save Caleb the son of Jephunneh, and Joshua the son of Nun. But your little ones, that ye said should be a prey, them will I bring in, and they shall know the land which ye have rejected. But as for you, your dead bodies shall fall in this wilderness. And your children shall be wanderers in the wilderness forty years, and shall bear your whoredoms, until your dead bodies be consumed in the wilderness. After the number of the days in which ye spied out the land, even forty days, for every day a year, shall ye bear your iniquities, even forty years, and ye shall know my alienation. I, Jehovah, have spoken, surely this will I do unto all this evil congregation, that are gathered together against me: in this wilderness they shall be consumed, and there they shall die."
Numbers 14:20-35

Of course, the backdrop of this story is, Moses led the Israelites out of Egypt, and they were traveling on what should have been an eleven-day journey towards the promised land. Nevertheless, they would not stop murmuring and complaining against the Lord. Numbers 14:1-4 gives us a little insight into what was going on. It reads, "And all the congregation lifted up their voice, and cried; and the people wept that night. And all the children of Israel murmured against Moses and against Aaron: and the whole congregation said unto them, Would that we had died in the land of Egypt! Or would that we had died in this wilderness! And wherefore doth Jehovah bring us unto this land, to fall by the sword? Our wives and our little ones will be a prey: were it not better for us to return into Egypt? And they said one to another, Let us make a captain, and let us return into Egypt."

God delivered the Jews from Egypt, but they were still soul-tied to their old season. For this reason, He sentenced them to forty years of wondering around in the wilderness. Some prophets and prophetic types enter caves because:

1. **They're still in love with their old seasons.** Like Jonah, they don't want to go forth, so they look for ways of escape. When this happens, God will often initiate a cave season or, better yet, a wilderness season designed to get the man or woman of God to stop looking back and start moving forward.
2. **They have not learned to bridle their tongues.** Complaining is on the opposite end of the spectrum from praying. Prayer is designed to move God, but complaining (if we're honest) is often our attempt to scare God into submission.

If you find yourself in this season, simply repent, surrender your heart to the Lord, submit your lips to the Lord and end your relationship with your last season.

#3 The Wilderness Cave

"Then was Jesus led up of the Spirit into the wilderness to be tempted of the devil. And when he had fasted forty days and forty nights, he afterward hungered. And the tempter came and said unto him, If thou art the Son of God,

command that these stones become bread. But he answered and said, It is written, Man shall not live by bread alone, but by every word that proceedeth out of the mouth of God. Then the devil taketh him into the holy city; and he set him on the pinnacle of the temple, and saith unto him, If thou art the Son of God, cast thyself down: for it is written, He shall give his angels charge concerning thee: and, On their hands they shall bear thee up, Lest haply thou dash thy foot against a stone.
Jesus said unto him, Again it is written, Thou shalt not make trial of the Lord thy God.
Again, the devil taketh him unto an exceeding high mountain, and showeth him all the kingdoms of the world, and the glory of them; and he said unto him, All these things will I give thee, if thou wilt fall down and worship me. Then saith Jesus unto him, Get thee hence, Satan: for it is written, Thou shalt worship the Lord thy God, and him only shalt thou serve. Then the devil leaveth him; and behold, angels came and ministered unto him."

Matthew 4:1-11

There will be seasons when the Lord may allow you to be tempted, but of course, with all temptation, He will give you a way of escape. Think about Joseph's encounter with Potiphar's wife. Joseph, in that moment, was being tempted by the devil. Sure, he saw what was likely a beautiful woman standing in front of him, but Joseph was an integral man. He couldn't imagine betraying the man who had favored him so much that he'd entrusted him with everything that he owned. Joseph was a man of gratitude, and for this reason, he found himself living a life of favor and luxury. But once he passed the test of temptation, he was lied on and thrown into prison to endure yet another test—the test of being forgotten.

Let's revisit the tests Jesus had to endure in the wilderness.

Jesus's first test was temptation. He was hungry, and the enemy saw this as an opportunity. Note: Satan cannot test you in an area that you're satisfied in.

His second test was suicide. Again, the enemy took Him to the holy city and sat Him on the pinnacle of a temple, and from there, he told Him, "If thou art the Son of God, cast thyself down: for it is written, He shall give his angels charge concerning thee: and, on their hands they shall bear thee up, Lest haply thou dash thy foot against a stone." The word *pinnacle* means the highest point. Just as he'd challenged Eve's identity, he was now in the midst of challenging the Lord's identity. Remember, this pinnacle was the very top of the Mountain of Religion.

The final test took place inside a cave. The scripture reads, "Again, the devil taketh him unto an exceeding high mountain, and showeth him all the kingdoms of the world, and the glory of them." Other translations use the word *into* instead of *unto*. Caves are hollow spots in the sides of mountains. The enemy took Jesus in a cave and began to test Him with His own possessions—the kingdoms of this world. This is what he does with believers to this day. He'll tempt a woman with a man that God has already approved for her life. He'll tempt the couple to fall into the trap of fornication, thinking it will strengthen their relationship when, in truth, it only serves to do the opposite.

To survive this season, you need to fast, pray and study your Word diligently. During this season, you may not be able to reach your multitude of counselors, but this is why you have to behave like the bear and fatten yourself up with the Word before this season hits. This way, when you find yourself in the midst of temptation, the Word will flow effortlessly from your lips, thus, causing the enemy to flee.

#4 The Cave of Restraint

"And she said unto him, How canst thou say, I love thee, when thy heart is not with me? thou hast mocked me these three times, and hast not told me wherein thy great strength lieth. And it came to pass, when she pressed him daily with her words, and urged him, that his soul was vexed unto death. And he told her all his heart, and said unto her, There hath not come a razor upon my head; for I have been a Nazirite unto God from my mother's womb: if I be shaven, then my strength will go from me, and I shall become weak, and be like any other man.
And when Delilah saw that he had told her all his heart, she sent and called for the lords of the Philistines, saying, Come up this once, for he hath told me all his heart. Then the lords of the Philistines came up unto her, and brought the money in their hand. And she made him sleep upon her knees; and she called for a man, and shaved off the seven locks of his head; and she began to afflict him, and his strength went from him. And she said, The Philistines are upon thee, Samson. And he awoke out of his sleep, and said, I will go out as at other times, and shake myself free. But he knew not that Jehovah was departed from him. And the Philistines laid hold on him, and put out his eyes; and they brought him down to Gaza, and bound him with fetters of brass; and he did grind in the prison-house. Howbeit the hair of his head began to grow again after he was shaven.
And the lords of the Philistines gathered them together to offer a great sacrifice unto Dagon their god, and to rejoice; for they said, Our god hath delivered Samson our enemy into our hand.
And when the people saw him, they praised their god; for they said, Our god hath delivered into our hand our enemy, and the destroyer of our country, who hath slain many of us. And it came to pass, when their hearts were merry, that they said, Call for Samson, that he may make us sport. And they called for Samson out of the prison-house; and he made

sport before them. And they set him between the pillars: and Samson said unto the lad that held him by the hand, Suffer me that I may feel the pillars whereupon the house resteth, that I may lean upon them. Now the house was full of men and women; and all the lords of the Philistines were there; and there were upon the roof about three thousand men and women, that beheld while Samson made sport.
And Samson called unto Jehovah, and said, O Lord Jehovah, remember me, I pray thee, and strengthen me, I pray thee, only this once, O God, that I may be at once avenged of the Philistines for my two eyes. And Samson took hold of the two middle pillars upon which the house rested, and leaned upon them, the one with his right hand, and the other with his left. And Samson said, Let me die with the Philistines. And he bowed himself with all his might; and the house fell upon the lords, and upon all the people that were therein. So the dead that he slew at his death were more than they that he slew in his life. Then his brethren and all the house of his father came down, and took him, and brought him up, and buried him between Zorah and Eshtaol in the burying-place of Manoah his father. And he judged Israel twenty years."

Judges 16:15-31

What is are troglobites again? "Troglobites are cave-dwelling creatures that navigate without eyes, go for weeks or months without food, and are believed to be able to exist for more than a hundred years."
(Source: English Word Information/ Word Info/ 2189)

Again, troglobites have no eyes, meaning, they are blind. They've been in the dark zone for so long that their eyes stopped developing. Samson was blind before the Philistines gouged his eyes out. As a matter of fact, this act of violence against him was symbolic of him choosing not to see the obvious. Samson was anointed, but carnal, and for this reason, he loved a godless woman. Nevertheless, after he was deceived and he'd realized the error of his ways, he decided that his last act would be to take vengeance against the Philistines.

This is important to note—it is possible to sit in the caves of obscurity for so long that you become as dark as the cave you're in. If you find yourself in this state—isolated because of sin or shame, the best way to come out of this cave is by simply repenting. To repent isn't just to apologize; in this, you have to do like Jonah did and finally agree to do God's will.

#5 The Cave of Rest

"And the Heavens and the Earth were finished, and all the host of them. And on the seventh day God finished his work which he had made; and he rested on the seventh day from all his work which he had made. And God blessed the seventh day, and hallowed it; because that in it he rested from all his work which God had created and made."

Genesis 2:1-3

You didn't create the night and the day, nor did you separate the two. You didn't create the waters or the firmament, nor have you split the Red Sea. You weren't the one who saved Jonah from the belly of the whale. You weren't the one who rescued David from Goliath, Saul or his son, Absalom. You didn't rescue Elijah from Jezebel's wrath. There's a lot that you have not done, but then again, you have been busy, and for this reason, God has carved out time for you to rest. Of course, I'm not just talking about the six to eight hours of sleep that you should be getting every night, I'm talking about you taking time off occasionally from everything except God, of course. After all, our jobs give us a certain amount of vacation days. Why is it that we think God is a task master? The answer is—we haven't sought Him like we should, and therefore, we don't know Him like we should.

Sometimes, God will call you to a cave just for you to rest. This cave season isn't super spiritual, nor is it designed to punish you. This is a time that the Lord has strategically mapped out for you to rest or be developed. Instead of ignoring your body and ignoring the voice of the Lord, tell yourself that it's okay for you to rest. You survive this season by simply turning down the volume on your cell phone and every voice that's trying to burn you out! This is your torpor state; this is your opportunity to recharge.

So, in summary, how does one handle being hidden?
1. **Find out who's hiding you.** Are you hiding yourself because of fear, offense or entitlement, or are you being called to a cave by the Lord? This will help you to discern whether you're entering a womb or a tomb.
2. **Utilize your multitude of counselors.** Be accountable with every prophetic message you receive, every feeling you have and every decision you make. A lot of prophets, prophetic types and other gifts go into caves of rebellion simply because someone offended them, someone prophesied to them or someone didn't give them the accolades they believe they are entitled to. You need sound, godly people who will hear your case and render righteous judgment regarding the matter.
3. **If you're in a cave, seek the presence of God with everything in you.** Don't throw away that season talking on the phone or inviting people to your cave. Caves are dark, caves are cold, and caves can be lonely. Let the glory of God fill that space, let the love of God be your warmth and learn to be satisfied with the presence of God.
4. **You're there to learn, not to complain!** Remember, you must come up to come out. This means that you have to allow the Word to mature you. Hear

me—there are prophets to this day who are trapped in cave seasons that they should have left thirty and forty years ago! How did they get stuck? They spent too much time trying to give a word, instead of investing time in receiving one. In other words, they became prideful, unteachable and religious. Anytime you enter a cave season and you don't learn anything in it or from it, you will inevitably have to return to that cave. You'll remain in that season until you get the lesson you are there to get.

5. **You may be in a state of torpor!** In other words, you may be able to briefly leave your cave to visit friends, go to events or to take a vacation. Hear me—it is not the will of God for you to sit in depression. This is why during these seasons, He'll often compel you to go to certain events, parties or visit certain individuals. This doesn't mean you've come out of your cave, it simply means you're stretching your legs outside of your cave.

6. **Get counseling!** There are some cave seasons when you just need a counselor. You don't need to over-spiritualize your dilemma or blame others for what you may be feeling. Get this—black bears and grizzly bears can be in a state of torpor for one hundred days and not have a single bowel movement! Can you imagine that?! Offense and fear are the waste of your soul! You shouldn't hold this stuff in for too long! Get counseling from a trained medical professional so that you can be emotionally healthy.

7. **Get regularly scheduled deliverance!** If you put a gift in a closet or an enclosed space for a long time, it's liable to get some dust or cobwebs on it. Before you present that gift to the receiver, you have to dust it off. You are a gift! Before God will present you to your next assignment, He wants to cleanse your soul. You should be submitting to deliverance at least

twice a year, especially if you are called to ministry.
8. **Learn to manage your soul.** We see examples of David doing this in Psalm 103:1 and Psalm 42:5. Remember, your soul is comprised of your mind, will and emotions. It is important that you learn to manage every aspect of yourself. Psalm 103:1 reads, "Bless the LORD, O my soul: and all that is within me, bless his holy name." In this, he was telling himself how to feel and how to behave, as opposed to allowing his feelings to become his guide. Psalm 42:5 reads, "Why art thou cast down, O my soul? And why art thou disquieted in me? Hope thou in God: for I shall yet praise him for the help of his countenance." 1 Samuel 30:6 reads, "And David was greatly distressed; for the people spake of stoning him, because the soul of all the people was grieved, every man for his sons and for his daughters: but David encouraged himself in the LORD his God."
9. **Put on and keep on the whole armor of God.** Ephesians 6:10-18 reads, "Finally, be strong in the Lord, and in the strength of his might. Put on the whole armor of God, that ye may be able to stand against the wiles of the devil. For our wrestling is not against flesh and blood, but against the principalities, against the powers, against the world-rulers of this darkness, against the spiritual hosts of wickedness in the Heavenly places. Wherefore take up the whole armor of God, that ye may be able to withstand in the evil day, and, having done all, to stand. Stand therefore, having girded your loins with truth, and having put on the breastplate of righteousness, and having shod your feet with the preparation of the gospel of peace; withal taking up the shield of faith, wherewith ye shall be able to quench all the fiery darts of the evil one. And take the helmet of salvation, and the sword of the Spirit, which is the

word of God: with all prayer and supplication praying at all seasons in the Spirit, and watching thereunto in all perseverance and supplication for all the saints."

10. **Be patient with God.** Two of the most effective traps of the enemy are discontentment and impatience. When these two link up, we end up with churches filled with evangelists sleeping with the folks they were supposed to be evangelizing, pastors berating their sheep and congregants who simply do not grow. The evidence that your cave season is coming to an end is when you start feeling constricted, impatient, overlooked and misunderstood. This is when you find yourself on the altar at church praying for others while you're bleeding. Hear me—blood was meant for the altar! So, don't give up, don't complain and don't curse your season! Praise God even louder, fast even longer and bless others even more! This is how you drown out the voice of the enemy and cause him to flee!

Remember this, being hidden simply means that there is something in you or about you that God wants to reveal, but in order for Him to do this, He has to develop you. In other words, He wants to use you. Just say yes to His will, stop questioning how He's going to do it or why He's doing it, and you will see the salvation of your God! Encourage yourself every day and commit within yourself that you will not give up, despite how hard life gets. God has great plans for you, but with greatness comes Goliaths, great fish and Pharaohs. All you have to do is remind yourself that every weapon formed against you *will not* and *cannot* prosper. When you come to believe this with your whole heart, you will laugh with God while those weapons are being formed. You'll laugh even harder when the enemy brandishes them. This is because you are God's gift to your generation, your family and the body of Christ, and as such, Satan has no legal rights to you. He has the ability to tempt you, but he doesn't have the power to touch you. God has split seas, cast down Jezebels and overthrown kingdoms just for you to be who He's designed you to be. Let Him develop you all the more so that you can blaze a trail for the next generation.

DIAGRAMS

Calling and Purpose

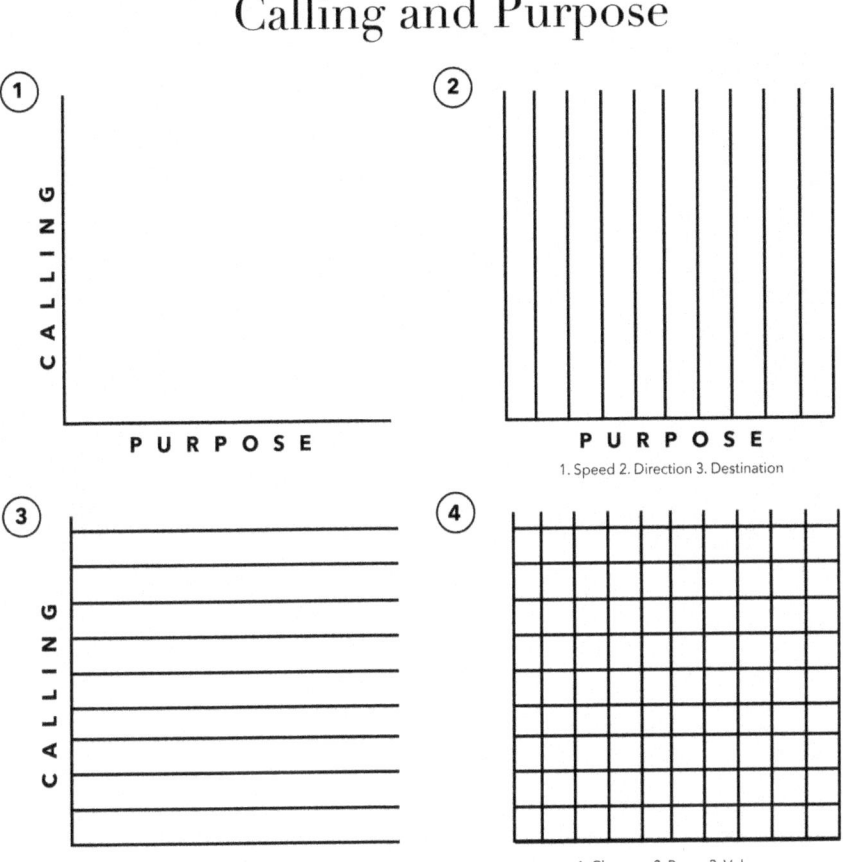

The Dynamics of a Dimension

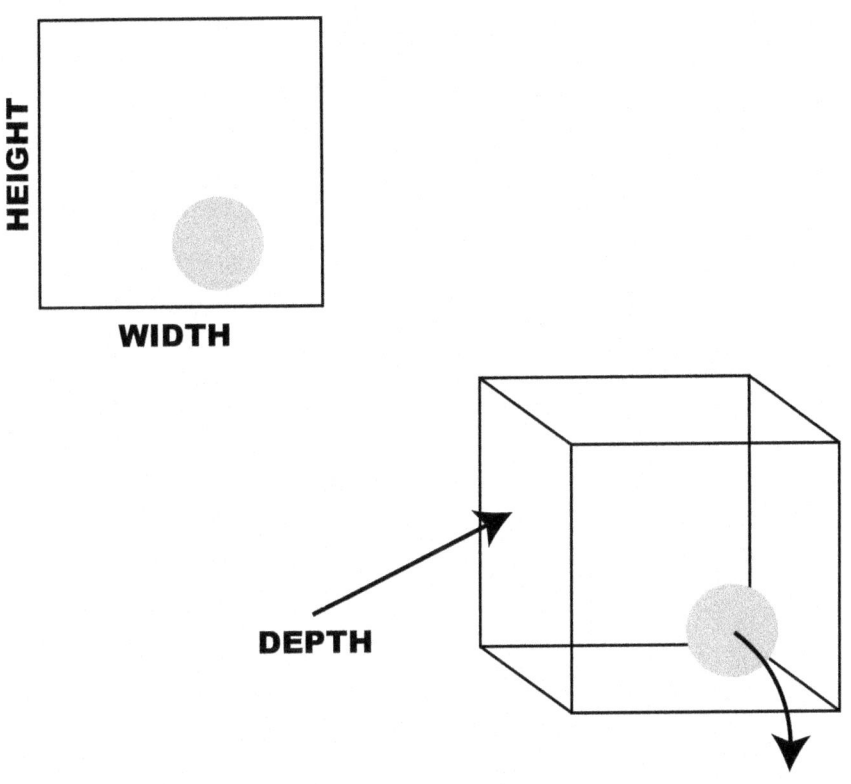

BRYAN MEADOWS MINISTRIES

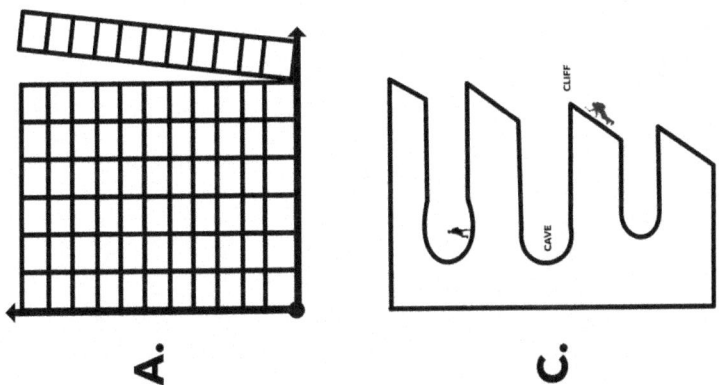

A.

B.

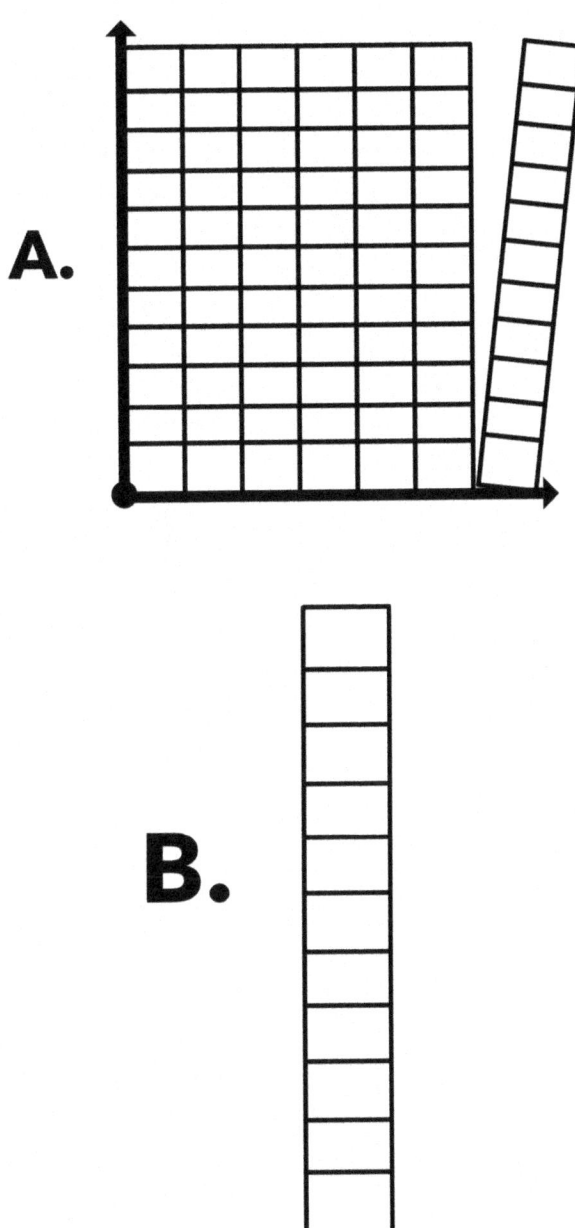

C.

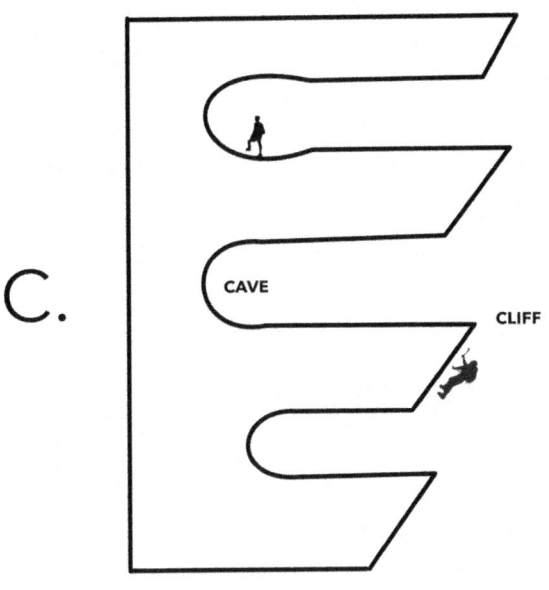

D.

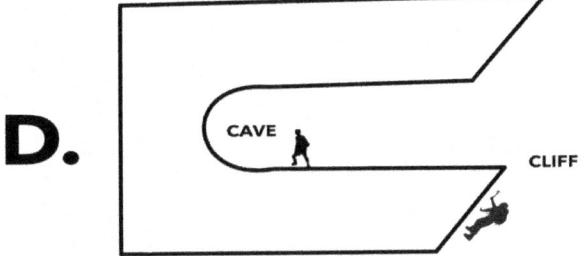

THE PURPOSE OF CAVES DIAGRAM

CLIFF
- BOUNDARIES

CAVE 4
- RECEIVE INSTRUCTION:
- LEAVE THE CAVE

CAVE 3
A PLACE OF TESTING:
- MIND
- HEART
- CHARACTER
- PROSPERITY

CAVE 2
A PLACE WHERE GOD SITS ON YOU:
- TO TURN
- DEVELOP
- GROW

CAVE 1
A PLACE OF TESTING:
WHERE GOD ELIMINATES YOUR COMPANY
TO CONCENTRATE ON HIM

LEVELS OF CAVES
- INSTRUCTION
- INSPIRATION
- INCUBATION
- ISOLATION

THE PURPOSE OF CAVES DIAGRAM

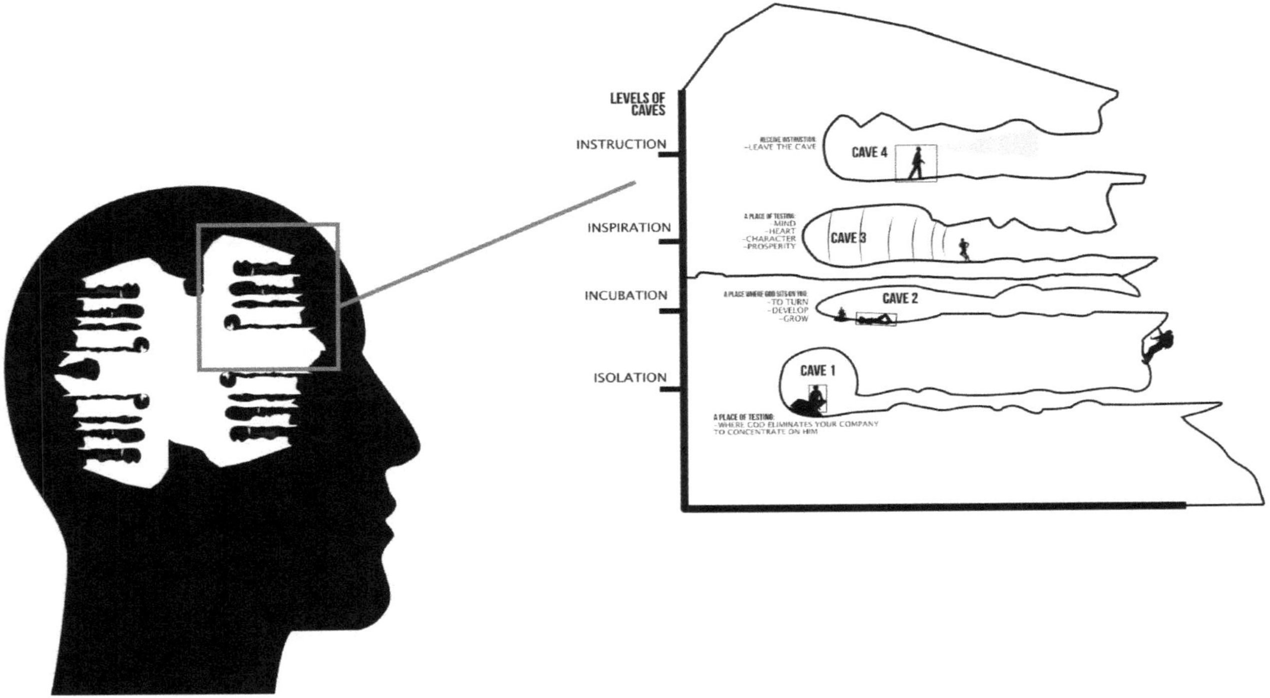

DEPTHS OF THE CAVE

CAVE ZONES

ENTRANCE ZONE
SUNLIGHT
VARIABLE TEMPERATURE
GREEN VEGETATION

TWILIGHT ZONE
LESS LIGHT
MINOR TEMPERATURE CHANGES
MINIMAL PLANT LIFE

DARK ZONE
NO LIGHT
CONSTANT TEMPERATURE
NO PLANT LIFE

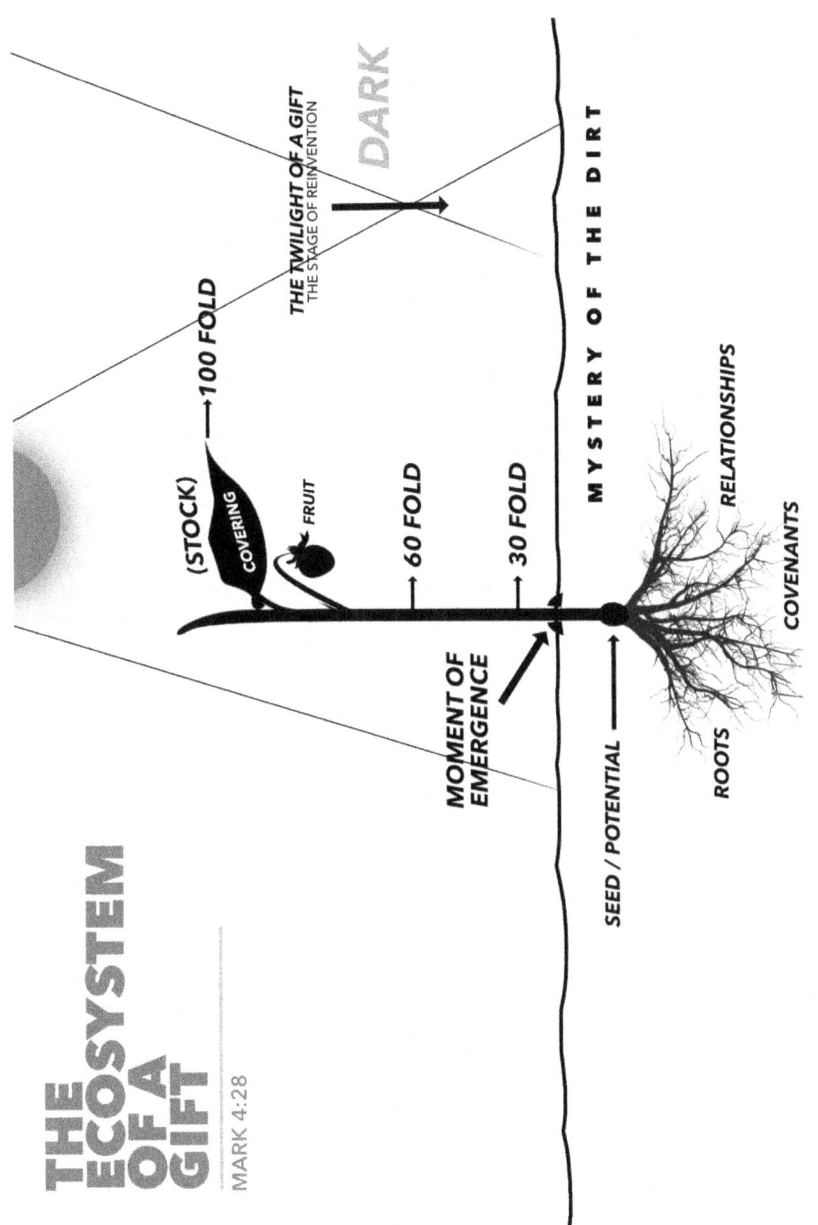

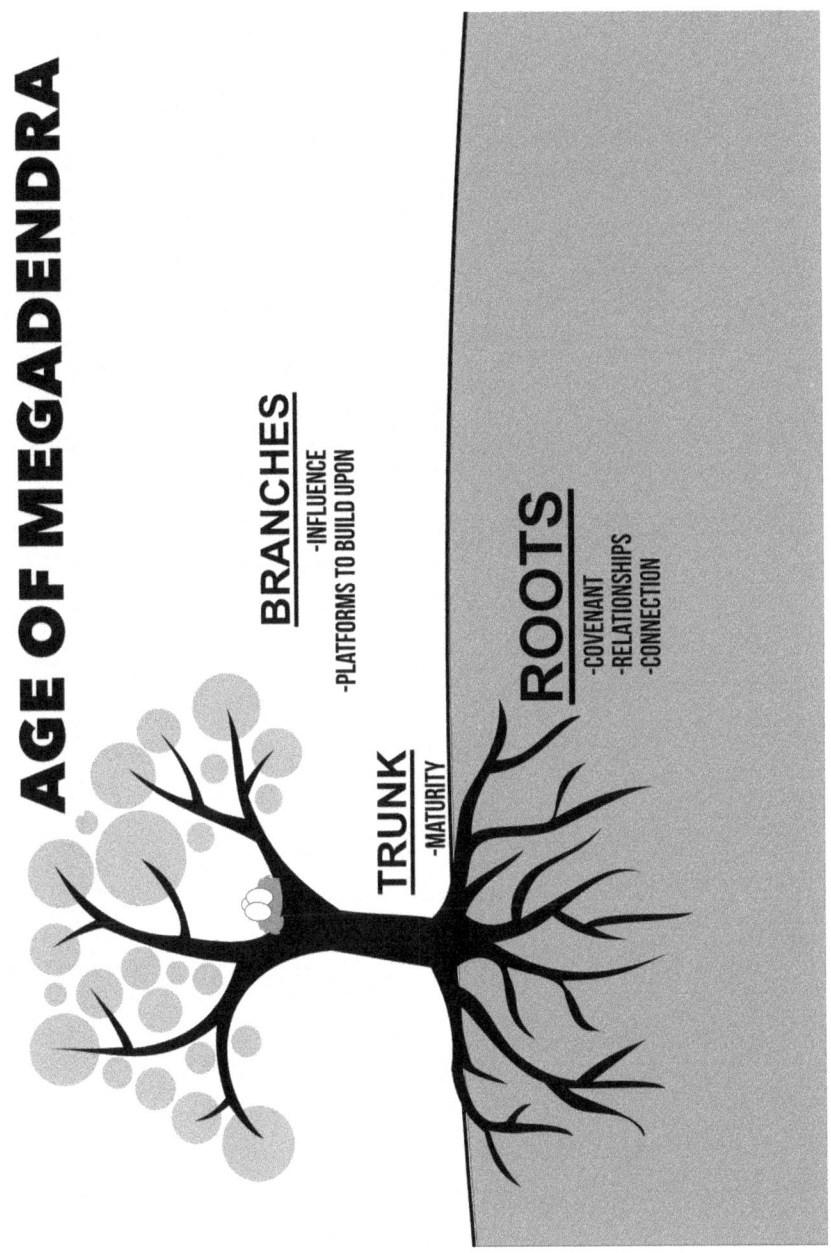

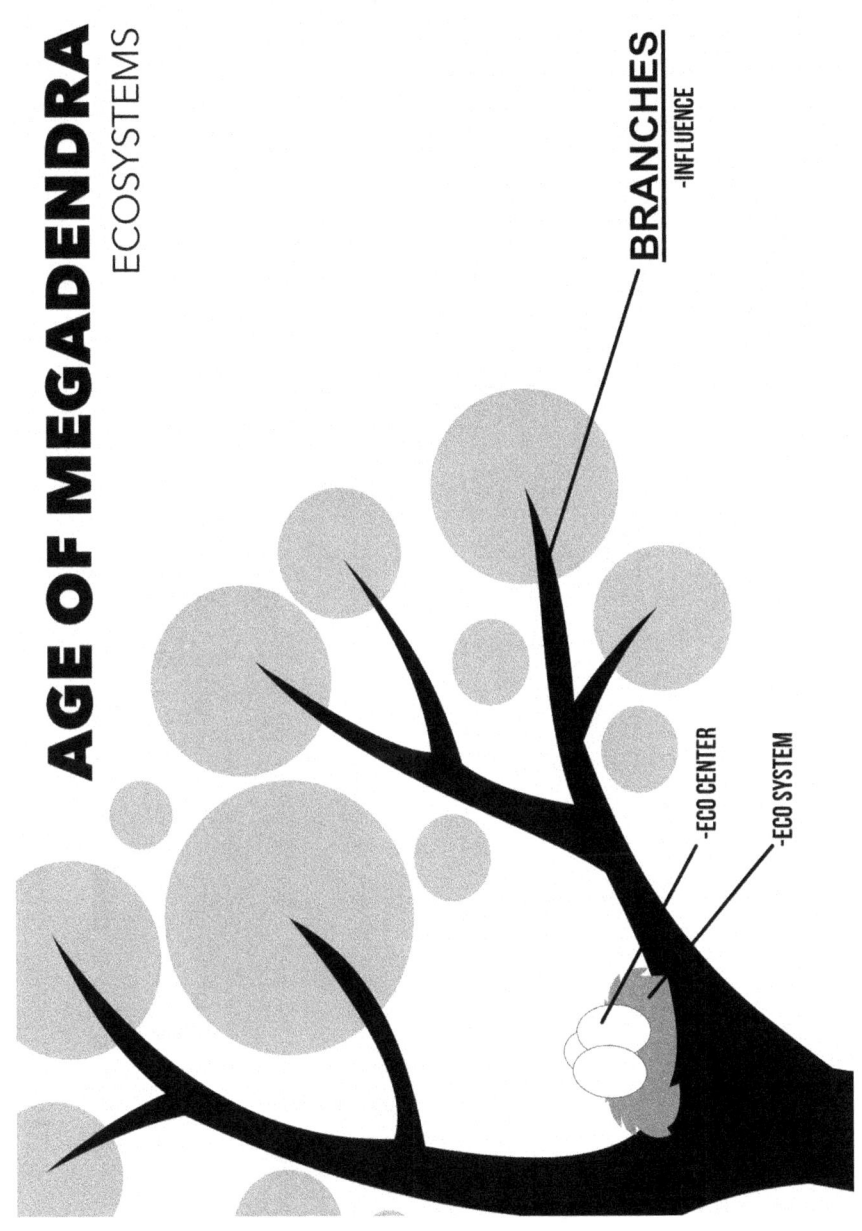

AGE OF MEGADENDRA
EAGLES EYE VIEW

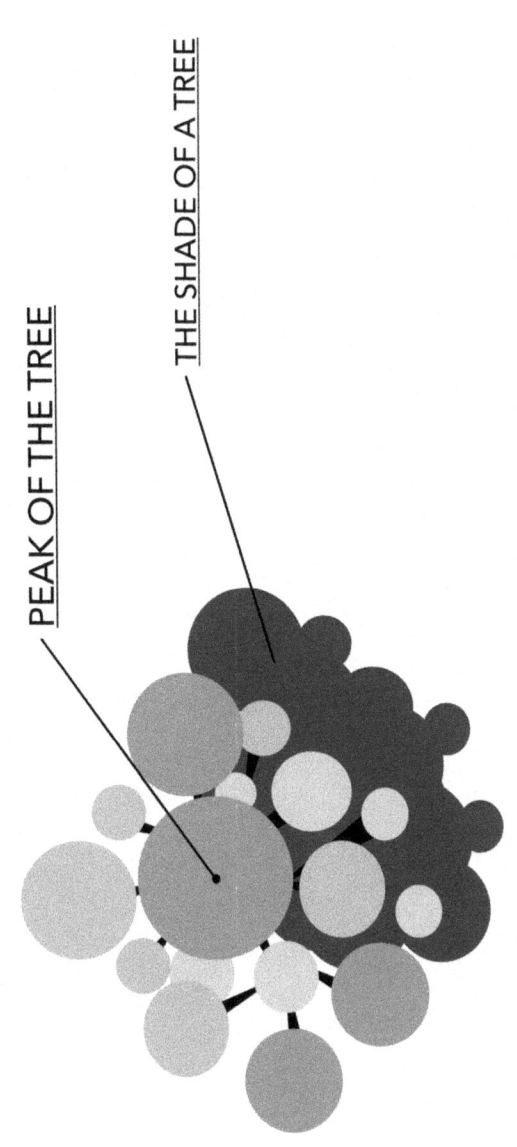

www.ingramcontent.com/pod-product-compliance
Lightning Source LLC
Chambersburg PA
CBHW071111160426
43196CB00013B/2540